THE SCOTTISH ELECTORATE

Also by Alice Brown, David McCrone and Lindsay Paterson

POLITICS AND SOCIETY IN SCOTLAND

Also by Alice Brown

CHANGING THE FACE OF PARTY POLITICS: A Major Crisis?
(*with Werner Bonefeld and Peter Burnham*)

Also by David McCrone

UNDERSTANDING SCOTLAND

SCOTLAND THE BRAND

THE SOCIOLOGY OF NATIONALISM: Tomorrow's Ancestors

Also by Lindsay Paterson

THE AUTONOMY OF MODERN SCOTLAND

A DIVERSE ASSEMBLY: The Debate on a Scottish Parliament

The Scottish Electorate

The 1997 General Election and Beyond

Alice Brown
Professor of Politics
University of Edinburgh

David McCrone
Professor of Sociology
University of Edinburgh

Lindsay Paterson
Professor of Educational Policy
Moray House Institute of Education
University of Edinburgh

and

Paula Surridge
Lecturer in Sociology
University of Aberdeen

First published in Great Britain 1999 by
MACMILLAN PRESS LTD
Houndmills, Basingstoke, Hampshire RG21 6XS and London
Companies and representatives throughout the world

A catalogue record for this book is available from the British Library.

ISBN 0–333–72525–5 hardcover
ISBN 0–333–72526–3 paperback

First published in the United States of America 1999 by
ST. MARTIN'S PRESS, INC.,
Scholarly and Reference Division,
175 Fifth Avenue, New York, N.Y. 10010

ISBN 0–312–21614–9

Library of Congress Cataloging-in-Publication Data
The Scottish electorate : the 1997 general election and beyond / Alice
Brown ... [et al.].
p. cm.
Includes bibliographical references and index.
ISBN 0–312–21614–9 (alk. paper)
1. Elections—Scotland. 2. Great Britain. Parliament—Elections,
1997. 3. Political parties—Scotland. 4. Scotland—Politics and
government. I. Brown, Alice, 1946– .
JN1341.S39 1998
324.9411'0859—dc21   98–15609
                                                                 CIP

This book is printed on paper suitable for recycling and made from fully managed and
sustained forest sources.

10 9 8 7 6 5 4 3 2 1
08 07 06 05 04 03 02 01 00 99

Printed and bound in Great Britain by
Antony Rowe Ltd, Chippenham, Wiltshire

Contents

List of Tables

Date of table is 1997 unless otherwise stated.

Preface

Scottish politics crossed a threshold in 1997. Not only was there a change of government – and not only was the Conservative Party left after the general election with no seats at all in Scotland – but there was also a referendum in which clear majorities voted to set up a Scottish Parliament and to give it some powers of taxation. As a result of these events, Scottish politics will never be the same again.

This book uses survey data to try to understand why these events took the form they did, and what they might lead to in the future. The analysis is the first full public airing of the data from the Scottish Election Survey and the Scottish Referendum Survey of 1997. The links between these and the British Election Survey allow comparisons to be drawn between Scotland and elsewhere, and the continuity with earlier surveys going back to 1974 allows some insights to be gained into how Scottish politics has been changing.

The first two chapters, however, do not use the surveys, but provide general context – of the distinctiveness of Scottish politics (Chapter One) and of the specific events between 1992 and the 1997 general election (Chapter Two). These chapters set the scene for the analysis of the survey data in the subsequent five chapters. Chapter Three analyses who voted for which party, and how these votes relate to such sociological variables as sex, age, social class, education, religion and identity. Chapter Four looks at people's political values and the effects of these on political behaviour; Chapter Five does likewise for people's preferences in policy. Chapter Six examines the referendum vote in detail, and Chapter Seven then uses the data to try to predict how Scottish politics will develop once the Scottish Parliament is set up in 1999. There is a technical Appendix at the end which describes the surveys in some more detail and explains the principles underlying the statistical techniques used in the text. Notes in the text have been kept to a minimum. References are grouped at the end of the book.

Acknowledgements

The book is a collaborative work to which each author contributed equally; the order of names on the title page reflects only the alphabet. John Curtice and Neil MacCormick made comments on drafts of all or parts of the text. The staff at Social and Community Planning Research, London (who conducted the Election and Referendum Surveys) have been helpful sources of advice, notably Roger Jowell, Alison Park, Bridget Taylor and Katarina Thomson. The Centre for Research into Elections and Social Trends (CREST, directed by John Curtice, Anthony Heath and Roger Jowell) provided many opportunities for discussion of the research, as did the Unit for the Study of Government in Scotland with the help of its administrator Lindsay Adams. In particular, Chapter Six has benefited from being the basis of a presentation to a conference on Understanding Constitutional Change in November 1997 (organised by the Unit and CREST, sponsored by BT and published as a special issue of the journal *Scottish Affairs* (Surridge et al, 1998)). A version of Chapter Two was published in the journal *Parliamentary Affairs* (Brown 1997). As detailed in the Appendix, the surveys were funded by the Economic and Social Research Council, to whom we are grateful.

1

Introduction: the Distinctiveness of Scottish Politics

INTRODUCTION

'There shall be a Scottish Parliament'. So began clause one of the 1997 Scotland Bill. The election of a Labour government in May 1997 with a record majority – after 18 years of Conservative rule – provided the opportunity for constitutional change which many political activists in Scotland had campaigned for over a long period of time. The White Paper on a Scottish Parliament published in July, soon after the election, corresponded very closely to the proposals for constitutional reform discussed and agreed during the years of the Scottish Constitutional Convention and contained in the Convention's final report, *Scotland's Parliament, Scotland's Right* (SCC, 1995). Anxieties were allayed surrounding Labour's decision in 1996 to hold a two-question referendum on a Scottish Parliament and on its proposed tax powers, if elected, as were fears that the party would not honour many of its pre-election promises on the issue (see Chapter Two). The results of the referendum which followed in September were, according to Donald Dewar, the Secretary of State for Scotland, beyond his wildest dreams. In accordance with the government's planned timetable, the Scotland Bill was published in December 1997 before being presented to the House of Commons in January 1998. The first elections were scheduled for May 1999 so that the Scottish Parliament could be fully operational from the year 2000. The setting up of a Parliament in Scotland, almost 300 years since the Treaty of Union, marks an important turning point and the beginning of another and significant phase in the development of Scottish politics.

This book provides an up-to-date assessment of Scottish electoral politics, setting the 1997 Scottish result in a comparative context with the rest of Britain, and in the context of changing political attitudes and behaviour since the 1970s. It draws on survey evidence from the 1997 Scottish Election Study in an attempt to understand the results of the general election and the referendum in Scotland, and to explore Scottish politics as Scotland moves towards a new constitutional future.

In this chapter we discuss the growing distinctiveness of Scottish politics and assess the possible impact of the establishment of a new Parliament on party politics, as well as the implications of introducing a new electoral system – the Additional Member System – for elections to the new Parliament. We consider the effects on the internal workings of the political parties in Scotland, and on the competition among them. Clearly, the rules and nature of the political game will be altered, probably resulting in a more pluralist political culture and system in Scotland.

Can we be sure, however, that radical change to the political culture will come about? Is it not the case that the Scottish electorate is best understood simply as a variety of the British electorate? That is not our view. The two central and connected themes in the electoral sociology of Scotland since 1945 have been:

- the growing divergence north and south of the border of the electoral performances of the Conservative and Labour Parties;
- the rise of a party seeking independence, the Scottish National Party.

Some critics, such as the historian Eric Hobsbawm, have argued that Scottish nationalism is simply the outcome of adverse political processes. It is, he comments, 'plainly a reaction to an all-British government supported by only a modest minority of Scots, and a politically impotent all-British opposition party' (1990, p.179), a state of affairs no doubt to be redressed by the election of a Labour government, when support for nationalism will, he assumes, ebb away. Events have proved him wrong. Support for a Scottish Parliament did not ebb away following Labour's stunning victory in May 1997. If anything it has grown since then, and with it support for the SNP. The creation of a Scottish Parliament and the opportunity for people in Scotland to vote separately for the Westminster and Scottish Parliaments in future, and to split their votes under a more proportional electoral system, will mean that the distinctive nature of Scottish politics is likely to grow.

PARTY POLITICS IN SCOTLAND

On the face of it, Scottish politics – with the exception of the SNP – look to be 'British with a difference' (McAllister and Rose, 1984, p.136). After all, the three other parties operate north and south of the border, and there seems nothing of the constitutional distinctiveness which exists across the North Channel in Northern Ireland. But to say this would be to assume that because the party labels were similar they operate with the same political agendas (although even the labels are not the same: they are called, after all, the Scottish Labour Party, the Scottish Conservative and Unionist party and the Scottish Liberal Democrats). To treat the United Kingdom as a unitary state in this way is to assume that the political system is unitary and homogeneous. The party labels may sound similar, but both the histories and agendas of the parties in the two parts of the kingdom are distinct (Miller, 1981; Johnson et al, 1988). We have argued elsewhere (Brown et al, 1996, 1998) that the Scottish parties are successful when they shape Scottish concerns to Westminster and vice versa in order to maximise Scottish influence.

The key to this is that the political parties have operated within a specific political context in Scotland. Although Scotland has not had its own Parliament since the Treaty of Union in 1707, it has enjoyed a distinctive level of autonomy over its own affairs (Paterson, 1994). Many histories of Scotland focus on three key institutions as forming the basis of Scottish autonomy, the so-called 'holy trinity' – the church, the legal system and education. The Presbyterian church provided a very distinctive religious and cultural element in Scottish life. Scotland retained its own legal system following the Union, and the education system developed along distinctly different lines from its

English counterpart. These three institutions helped form and develop a distinctive Scottish national identity and context, but there are other key institutions and features that are often overlooked. Scotland has a separate local government system, a distinctive trade union movement, business and financial community, press and broadcasting media, and a whole host of other organisations and pressure groups with a specifically Scottish focus. These are expressions of a distinctive civil society, with its own self-regulating institutions.

Over the past hundred years, however, Scottish political and administrative affairs have been managed within the British system through the Scottish Office, established in 1885, and headed by a Scottish Secretary of State, a post with a seat in the Cabinet since 1926. Recognition of Scotland's position in the United Kingdom as one of its founding partners is further demonstrated by the disproportionate number of MPs representing Scotland at Westminster, and the role given to the Scottish Grand Committee and Scottish Affairs Committee in the House of Commons. It is within this distinctive context that Scottish political identity has developed and in which the parties operate north of the border.

That is why Scotland is not a 'region' of the United Kingdom. The Treaty of Union of 1707 marked what we might term the marriage of convenience between Scotland and England for whom it served different but mutually compatible ends. The development of Scottish autonomy and this 'negotiated compromise' marked the relationship between Scotland and England from the eighteenth century, through the era of the legal state in the nineteenth century and the technocratic state of the twentieth century (Paterson, 1994). In the nineteenth century the government of Scotland consisted of a network of local councils and national boards staffed by the professional middle-class and led by the legal profession. The network of elites was responsible for a range of policy areas and operated on the basis of conventions and traditions. In this period, the United Kingdom was one of the most decentralised states in Europe and there was little interference in Scottish affairs from British politicians. During the century which followed, the belief in technical solutions to political problems developed, providing a more central role for bureaucrats in the system of government. It is in this period that the Scottish Office gained greater autonomy and powers and operated within a framework of informal rules in collaboration with a policy network of professionals. The system retained its legitimacy up to the 1970s because Scotland had significant control over its administrative politics and the scope for exercising its own choices in domestic policies. The system was severely tested, however, in the period that followed, especially with the election of the Conservative government in 1979 led by Margaret Thatcher. In this new context, pressure on the 'negotiated compromise' grew, and policy-making in Scotland came under significant strain (Brown et al, 1996, 1998).

Another distinctive feature of the Scottish political system is, of course, that Scotland has four main political parties, not three. The existence of a nationalist party, the SNP, provides an added dimension to inter-party relationships and competition. While the SNP injects an obvious and explicit 'nationalist' agenda into Scottish politics, it is important to remember that in a crucial sense Scottish politics have always been nationalist insofar as Scotland's interests have always been paramount in explaining the success and failure of the parties. Scotland's relative autonomy within the UK has meant that parties are successful when they defend and extend this autonomy. All three 'non-nationalist' parties have succeeded in this at different points in history: the Liberals in the nineteenth century, the Tories in the first half of the twentieth century, and Labour for much of the second half. Where these parties falter, as they began to do in the final quarter of this century, political space opens up for a fourth, explicitly nationalist, party, the SNP. In many respects, the apparent dominance by one or other party is a function of a four-party system operating within first-past-the-post electoral politics. Hence the Labour Party has enjoyed considerable hegemony and is the dominant party in local government, at Westminster and in the European Parliament (Lynch, 1996a).

If we take the long view of Scottish politics, we can identify four key dates in political history. The first is 1832, the date of the Reform Acts which was followed by a long period of Liberal Party hegemony in Scotland. The year 1886 marked the second period when the new political force of Unionism, capitalising on the split within the Liberals over Irish home rule, turned out to dominate politics in Scotland for the following 50 years. By 1922, the Labour Party had asserted itself as the main opposition to Unionism, replacing the Liberal Party in the process. Labour did not come to dominate Scottish politics in the way the Liberals did in the previous century, but they did provide the opposition to a Scottish Conservative and Unionist party which uniquely achieved over 50 per cent of the popular vote in the general election of 1955, the only party to do so in Scotland since 1945. The fourth key date in Scottish politics came at the October 1974 general election, when the SNP broke through to achieve its highest electoral support to date at a general election, winning 30 per cent of the popular vote and 11 Parliamentary seats, and thus identifying itself as a major challenge to the Labour Party in Scotland. If 1832, 1886, 1922 and 1974 represent major caesura in Scottish politics, then the year 1999 will be another significant year with the election of the first Scottish Parliament for almost 300 years.

The context for these forthcoming changes is the changing electoral fortunes of the parties in the post-1945 period. Support for the political parties has shifted over this half-century. Table 1.1 shows the number of seats won by the different parties and their percentage share of the vote in Scotland at general elections since 1945.

We can see the way in which the first-past-the-post system has worked very much in favour of the Labour Party, as well as the dramatic decline in support for the Conservative Party from the mid-1950s onwards. Labour succeeded under the current system in winning 56 of the 72 seats in Scotland in 1997. That is, with less than half of the popular vote, Labour obtained more than three-quarters of the seats. Conservative Party support, on the other hand, has declined significantly. While it took over 50 per cent of the vote and 36 seats in 1955, it reached an all-time low level of 17.5 per cent of the vote and no seats at all in the 1997 general election. Both the Scottish Liberal Democrats and the SNP have been victims of the electoral system as the third and fourth parties in a four-party system. Nevertheless, with careful targeting of their support, the Liberal Democrats succeeded in obtaining ten seats in 1997 with just 13 per cent of the vote, while the SNP achieved only six seats in spite of gaining over 22 per cent of the vote.

These results would be remarkable enough in themselves, but by setting them in the context of election results south of the border, we

Table 1.1:   Votes and seats in Scotland, general elections,   1945-1997

	Percentage of vote (number of seats)				
Year	Labour	Conserv-ative	Liberal	SNP	Other
1945	47.6 (37) 1.8 (3) ILP	41.1 (27)	5.0	1.2	3.3 (4)
1950	46.2 (37)	44.8 (32)	6.6 (2)	0.4	1.6
1951	47.9 (35)	48.6 (35)	2.7 (1)	0.3	0.5
1955	46.7 (34)	50.1 (36)	1.9 (1)	0.5	0.8
1959	46.7 (38)	47.2 (31)	4.1 (1)	0.5	1.2
1964	48.7 (43)	40.6 (24)	7.6 (4)	2.4	0.7
1966	49.9 (46)	37.7 (20)	6.8 (5)	5.0	0.6
1970	44.5 (44)	38.0 (23)	5.5 (3)	11.4 (1)	0.6
1974 (Feb)	36.6 (41)	32.9 (21)	8.0 (3)	21.9 (7)	0.6
1974 (Oct)	36.3 (41)	24.7 (16)	8.3 (3)	30.4 (11)	0.3
1979	41.5 (44)	31.4 (22)	9.0 (3)	17.3 (2)	0.8
1983	35.1 (41)	28.4 (21)	24.5 (8)	11.7 (2)	0.3
1987	42.4 (50)	24.0 (10)	19.2 (9)	14.0 (3)	0.3
1992	39.0 (49)	25.7 (11)	13.1 (9)	21.5 (3)	0.8
1997	45.6 (56)	17.5 (0)	13.0 (10)	22.1 (6)	1.9

Source: Brown et al, 1998.

are able to judge their significance. There is an obvious divergence in voting behaviour between Scotland and England, most notably the decline of the Scottish Conservatives at a time when their English counterparts were flourishing. Table 1.2 illustrates the difference in support for the Conservative Party north and south of the border.

This divergence in voting patterns is dramatic. There has been a systematic swing away from the Conservatives and towards Labour in Scotland, excepting the period of the SNP surge from 1966 up to and

Table 1.2:   Conservative Party share of the vote,
              England and Scotland, general elections,
              1945-1997

| Year | *Conservative percentage of vote* | |
	England	Scotland
1945	40	41
1950	44	45
1951	49	49
1955	50	50
1959	50	47
1964	44	41
1966	43	38
1970	48	38
1974 (Feb)	40	33
1974 (Oct)	39	25
1979	47	31
1983	46	28
1987	46	24
1992	47	26
1997	34	18

Source: Brown et al, 1998.

including 1974. However, the move away from the Tories has been much more pronounced and consistent than the swing to Labour, for at one time or another all the non-Conservative parties have been beneficiaries of the anti-Tory vote, most spectacularly in 1997. The decline of the Conservatives and the rise of the SNP are connected by 'nationalism', and in the period running up to the 1997 general election the agenda of Scottish politics was increasingly shaped by nationalist concerns. These concerns were clearly permeating the Labour Party and the Liberal Democrats, as well as the SNP itself; the

Conservatives struggled to avoid being seen as an anti-Scottish party. The consequence of this pervasive nationalism was that all parties sought to be identifiably Scottish – Labour and the Liberal Democrats by adopting policies of home rule, and the Conservatives by trying to resurrect their own identity as the party of Scottish patriotism within the Union. The non-Conservative parties also attempted to distance themselves from a Euro-sceptic Conservative government by becoming increasingly European in their outlook. The outcome of the general election on the 1 May meant that for the first time in the country's history Scotland did not return a single Conservative MP. Neither did Wales. So the Conservatives ceased to be a British party, and were reduced to a rump representing mainly rural and suburban England.

THE PARTIES AND THE CONSTITUTION

As the Scottish and English electorates diverged, especially so far as voting Conservative was concerned, so the constitutional question grew in importance throughout the 1980s and 1990s. In the ways we have seen, this divergence predated the election of Conservative administrations since 1979, and in its origin cannot be attributed to the rightwards shift in the Tory party. Nevertheless, and given the size of the Scottish electorate compared to the English one, this divergence allowed opponents of the government and supporters of home rule to claim that Scotland had suffered a 'democratic deficit' in the sense that it was subject to policies for which it had not voted during the years of the Thatcher and Major administrations. Scotland had always seen itself as a partner, albeit a junior one, in creating and maintaining the United Kingdom, but such a view could not be sustained in the context of this democratic deficit, apparently driven home by the Scottish Office's being occupied by the handful of Conservatives who held Scottish seats.

Lessons from the experiences of the 1970s were drawn, especially from the referendum held by the Labour Party on constitutional reform in 1979 and the failure then to meet the requirement that 40 per cent of the whole electorate had to vote in favour before an elected Scottish Assembly would be set up. A wide range of groups emerged to take forward the campaign for home rule including the Campaign for a

Scottish Assembly (later to change its name to the Campaign for a Scottish Parliament – CSP) which was instrumental in establishing the Scottish Constitutional Convention in 1989, and the Coalition for Scottish Democracy which in turn set up the Scottish Civic Assembly in 1994. The final report of the Convention and the proposals contained within it were influential in the development of the Labour Party's policies for constitutional reform. The Convention was a cross-party body which worked in conjunction with a broad range of groups and organisations representing Scottish civil society. Neither the SNP nor Conservatives were members – the former, under the influence of its fundamentalist wing, because it considered that the Convention would be dominated by the Labour Party, and the Tories because they opposed any constitutional reform which required a directly elected Assembly or Parliament.

After six years of collaborative working and consensus-building, the Convention put forward its plans for a Scottish Parliament with 129 members (MSPs) elected by a variant of the Additional Member System (AMS): 73 constituency MSPs would be elected by first-past-the-post (Orkney and Shetland having been divided into two constituencies) and 56 additional MSPs would be elected from top-up lists (seven from each of Scotland's eight European constituencies). These proposals were endorsed in the Labour government's White Paper on a Scottish Parliament published in July 1997 and in the Scotland Bill published in December of the same year (and are discussed further below).

The White Paper set out the powers to be retained at Westminster under Labour's scheme (including foreign policy, defence, macro-economic policy and social security), stating that all areas not reserved would come under the power of the Scottish Parliament. These included a range of domestic responsibilities, such as health, education, training, local government, social work, housing, economic development, transport, law and home affairs, environment, agriculture, fisheries and forestry, sports and the arts, and research and statistics. Radical aspects of Labour's plans include the acceptance of the Convention's proposals to elect MSPs by the Additional Member System and an encouragement to parties to work towards better gender balance in representation. The White Paper stated that 'the government attach great importance to equal opportunities for all – including women, members of ethnic minorities and disabled people', and it urged 'all political parties offering candidates for election to the Scottish Parliament to have this in mind in their internal candidate selection processes' (Scottish Office, 1997). Other important factors include the power given to the Parliament to increase or decrease by up to three pence in the pound the basic rate of income tax set by the UK Parliament; this will provide some scope for the parties in the Parliament to gear their policies towards hypothecated taxation. Another is in the area of Parliamentary arrangements where the government proposes that standing orders should be designed to ensure openness, responsiveness and accountability and where Parliamentary committees may be given the power to initiate legislation in addition to their ability to scrutinise and amend. If the participation and involvement of organisations and individuals other than the political parties in decision-making is realised, then, in conjunction with a more proportional electoral system, this could help to bring about power-sharing.

The conversion of the Labour Party from a sceptical position to one of fulsome support for home rule was achieved by means of the Constitutional Convention. Together with its Liberal Democrat partners in the Convention, Labour grew to champion the cause, safe in the knowledge that its rivals the SNP had absented themselves from the Convention in 1989, considered by some commentators as a tactical political mistake. In spite of its distinctive policy of independence in Europe, the SNP decided to join the broad campaign organised by Scotland Forward in the run-up to the referendum. This decision was not met with unanimous approval by all political activists, the tension between the gradualist and fundamentalist wings within the party being exposed over the issue. But the policy of playing a constructive role in the Parliament in order to provide a 'stepping stone' to independence prevailed. Although there were different views within the Conservative Party north and south of the border, the official policy of the party was to campaign for a double 'No' vote. Opponents of constitutional change within the party warned of the danger of embarking on the 'slippery slope' to independence.

The experience of three political parties working together in Scotland Forward to make the case for constitutional reform was an unusual one in Scottish politics and was taken to be a demonstration of consensus and 'new' politics in Scotland (Jones, 1997; Pattie et al, 1998). Taking forward the spirit of cross-party co-operation, the Secretary of State, Donald Dewar, announced that he had issued invitations to the four main political parties, the Scottish Constitutional Convention and the Convention of Scottish Local Authorities to participate in a Consultative Steering Group to examine the Parliament's procedures. The group began its work in January 1998 – not without some strain in this new-found political consensus – and was asked to report to the Secretary of State by December of the same year in time for election year 1999.

NEW PARLIAMENT: NEW POLITICS?

The 1997 general election and referendum have had different effects on the different political parties in Scotland in terms of their internal relationships, their relationships with each other and, where relevant, their relationships with their British counterparts. Having absorbed the results of the general election, the parties began to turn to what the new political system would mean, and, in particular, the possible impact of the use of the Additional Member System for the first elections.

Elections to the Scottish Parliament

The implementation of the AMS for the elections is likely to have a significant effect on the hegemony that the Labour Party has enjoyed in Scottish politics in the last two decades. As Donald Dewar (1998, p.9) has acknowledged:

> The changes to the electoral system are by any standards brave and, indeed, some of my less charitable party colleagues regard the proportional electoral system as a form of charitable giving almost without precedent in Scottish politics.

He also went on to add that the proposed system should ensure fairer representation of women, of people from ethnic minorities and of other groups, and that no minority in Scotland would fail to get representation.

The electoral system will work as follows. Each elector will have two votes, one for a constituency MSP (current Westminster constituencies) and the other for a party (on the basis of Euro-constituencies). The constituency MSP will be elected by the present first-past-the-post system, while the second – party – vote will correct for disproportionality in the constituency section. In each Euro-constituency, votes for each party will be counted and divided by the number of constituency MSPs elected for each party, plus one. The party with most votes after this calculation gains the first additional member. The second to the seventh additional members are allocated in the same way, with additional members gained being included in the calculation. Let us take an example: suppose that in a Euro-constituency Labour takes five constituency seats, SNP two, and Liberal Democrats two, with Conservatives none. Labour's vote is divided by six (5+1), SNP and Liberal Democrats by three each (2+1). Whichever party has the highest vote after the total vote is divided by the number of seats won would get the first additional seat and so on, until the total number of seats had been allocated.

What is the likely outcome? Calculations based on the 1997 general election results demonstrated that Labour had made a major concession in agreeing to a more proportional system, as it effectively conceded an overall majority (Table 1.3).

Table 1.3:   Votes for Scotland's first Parliament

Party	Number of Seats	Direct+Additional
Labour	63	56+7
SNP	28	6+22
Conservative	22	0+22
Liberal Democrat	16	10+6
Total	129	

Assumes percentage share of the vote as at 1997 general election and no splitting of vote between the constituency and party votes.

The AMS system is not strictly proportional, for Labour wins nearly 49 per cent of the seats on less than 46 per cent of the vote, leaving them two seats short of an overall majority in the Scottish Parliament. That might actually be enough to allow them to form a reasonably robust minority government. Labour's advantage derives from the fact that 56 of its 63 MSPs would be elected by the first-past-the-post system. The AMS clearly corrects in favour of the Conservatives who would win all their seats by this means, and to a lesser extent the SNP who would gain 22 of their 28 seats in this way. Ironically, the Liberal Democrats, who have long been the advocates of proportionality, would drop from second to fourth place in the party rankings compared with their current share of Westminster MPs. Although Labour are correct in pointing out that by introducing a measure of proportional representation they are reducing their chances of winning power, if they were to poll at least as well as they did in 1997, when they won 45.6 per cent of the vote, then they would have a fair chance of forming a single party government if they so desired. Taking the 1992 election results as a rough guide of changing electoral fortunes, we find that Labour would have 54 seats, the Conservatives 30, the SNP 28 and the Liberal Democrats 17.

What makes elections for a Scottish Parliament far less predictable is that one cannot assume that Labour would do as well as they did in Scotland in 1997. Opinion polls since May 1997 suggest that Scottish voters are less likely to vote for Labour in a Scottish election than in a Westminster one. In all cases, the SNP is likely to be the beneficiary.

The second assumption which might be unwarranted is that voters would keep to the party slates for both directly elected and party list candidates. Tactical voting has been a feature of Scottish politics for some time – with the clearest effects in 1997 – and the new system provides electors with additional weapons of choice. We might even see voters using their 'direct' vote tactically because they are able to plump for particular candidates whereas the parties themselves will control the lists. In rural areas where there is a stronger tradition of voting for a particular candidate, this might encourage tactical voting for first-past-the-post candidates, and party preference on the second vote. In other words, we cannot be at all certain as to how the new electoral system will determine the outcome.

Since the election, opinion pollsters have been trying to assess how people will vote in the new system. While Labour maintains a healthy lead over their nearest opponents, the SNP, in votes for Westminster (around 20 percentage points in the first half of 1998), for a Scottish Parliament their lead is, at most, substantially less. In February 1998, for example, the System Three poll for *The Herald* gave Labour a 25 point lead over the SNP in a general election, but only a 11 point lead in Scottish Parliamentary elections. In the following two months, Labour and SNP were neck-and-neck, while their lead for Westminster elections held at 18 and 20 per cent. In June, the SNP was actually ahead of Labour for the Scottish Parliament (by 44 to 35), but still trailed them by 17 points for Westminster. Because of Labour's lead in the first-past-the-post seats in a Scottish Parliament election, they would still be likely to be the largest party even if they tied with the SNP in share of the vote, but they would be a long way short of an overall majority.

We cannot assume, moreover, that people will cast their second vote in the same way as their first. The ICM May 1998 poll found that 42 per cent would vote for Labour with their first vote, and 36 per cent for the SNP. (Voting for Westminster would put Labour on 47 per cent and the SNP on 27 per cent.) However, on the second vote, the SNP would take 39 per cent and Labour 36 per cent. This is because 30 per cent of Labour voters would switch to the SNP on the second vote (with 60 per cent intending to vote Labour twice), whereas only 20 per cent of SNP voters would reciprocate by voting Labour (67 per cent would intend to vote for the SNP on both votes). Translated into seats, this would give Labour 55, and the SNP 52, with the Liberal Democrats on 12, and the Tories on 10. Labour would need to govern with another party (probably the Liberal Democrats) to have an overall majority. Similarly, the SNP could only form a Scottish government if it too was in coalition, again with the Liberal Democrats as the likely candidates.

The data from the polls suggests that Scottish voters will behave in line with electors in other countries that have decentralised or devolved political systems. In Catalunya, for example, the

Nationalists take around 40 per cent of the votes in autonomous elections, and the Socialists 25 per cent, positions which are reversed in elections for the all-Spain Cortes. In like manner, people in Scotland are likely to use their votes in quite a sophisticated manner and to differentiate between elections for the Westminster Parliament and those for the Scottish Parliament. In addition, as is the case in other countries with Additional Member Systems, there is likely to be some splitting of votes between the constituency and additional seats (Boston et al, 1997).

Evidence from the study conducted by Dunleavy et al (1997) provides further support for the view that the introduction of the AMS in the first elections in Scotland is likely to have a significant impact on the distribution of seats won by the parties. The authors carried out simulations of elections using AMS based on the actual election results in 1997 and on opinion polls carried out by ICM research immediately after the election. Under one scenario, where people vote in the Scottish Parliament elections exactly as they did in the 1997 general election under first-past-the-post, and where their constituency and regional-level votes are identical, the authors calculate that Labour would win 62 seats, the SNP 29, the Conservatives 22 and the Liberal Democrats 16. These calculations correspond almost exactly with Table 1.3 above. Using a second scenario, they calculated people's votes for candidates at constituency and regional level in line with their responses to the ICM survey where respondents could engage in 'ticket-splitting'. Quite different results emerge from this exercise with both Labour and the Conservatives losing seats to the SNP and the Liberal Democrats. The survey suggests that Labour would win 58 seats, the SNP 37, the Liberal Democrats 21 and the Conservatives 13.

Conducting a similar exercise for Wales and commenting on the results of the second scenario, Dunleavy et al (1997) note 'a powerful effect which will create much more multi-party legislatures than the Labour government at Westminster expects'. However, although Labour would still have a majority of Assembly members in Wales under either scenario, this is unlikely to be the case for Labour in Scotland. Instead, a coalition of Labour and the Liberal Democrats seems the most likely outcome under either configuration of seats, with the SNP emerging as the main opposition party. While in Wales the elections to the new legislature may not affect the party system, the authors argue that in Scotland 'an increasing divide may open up between a Scottish party system and UK politics'. Thus in Scotland, Labour and the Liberal Democrats could sustain majority support, with the SNP the major opposition and the Conservatives pushed to the sidelines. In contrast, for the Westminster elections the Conservatives might return to being the main opposition to Labour with the SNP doing less well.

As opinion polls in late 1997 and early 1998 suggested closer competition between the Labour Party and the SNP, speculation about the 'stepping stone' or 'slippery slope' to independence has re-emerged. The results have also put pressure on the tactical consensus between the parties which emerged during the referendum campaign, with old rivalries being expressed. The SNP have raised the possibility of holding a referendum on independence during the first term of the Scottish Parliament, a suggestion that did not endear them to the other parties, especially the Scottish Liberal Democrats who would be their most likely coalition allies.

The Political Parties and Party Competition

Following the 1997 general election, and for quite different reasons, both the Scottish Labour Party and the Scottish Conservative and Unionist Party began to consider ways of reforming their constitutions and their relationships with their British parties.

The wipe-out of Conservatives MPs in Scotland had a devastating effect on the party which then had little chance of mounting a credible opposition to the referendum campaign organised by Scotland Forward. In any event, it appeared that voters in Scotland had already made up their minds in favour of constitutional reform (Jones, 1997; Pattie et al, 1998). Opinion polls over the summer of 1997 showed that once again the party was out of step with public opinion in Scotland in deciding to campaign against the government's home rule plans. As we will see in Chapter Six, the Conservatives lost support in the general election because of their stance on the constitution.

Even before the general election in May 1997 there were divisions within the party over the constitutional question and signs of plans to break away to form a separate organisation to fight elections for the expected Scottish Parliament. In the wake of the election defeat and the referendum there were renewed calls to accept the result and seize the opportunity which the Scottish Parliament would provide for the party. It is one of the ironies of politics that the Scottish Conservatives who had opposed the establishment of a Scottish Parliament and who had opposed proportional representation should then plan their revival in Scotland through the new institution with a new electoral system.

The Conservative response to electoral defeat was to set up a Commission to report on the future structure of the Scottish party; it reported to a special conference in February 1998. It recommended that the party chairman would be jointly appointed by elected members of the new national executive and the party leader; that a new and clearer management structure would be put in place; and that candidate selection would be conducted in Scotland and members would be involved in creating party lists for the Scottish and European Parliaments. In launching the report, the party leadership contrasted their approach to devolving power within the party to what they considered to be the centralist tendencies of New Labour. Launching another Commission to draw up a radical policy programme for the Scottish Parliament, the former Foreign Secretary and current President of the Scottish Conservatives, Sir Malcolm Rifkind, stated that it was the second phase of a three-stage 'renaissance' of the Conservatives north of the border. The first phase involved a restructuring of the party into one organisation and the third would be to present its new policies to the public.

The establishment of a Parliament in Scotland also offers new challenges to the Scottish Labour Party. Again, before the general election, changes within the party were already taking place, especially in the composition of the Scottish executive in the spring of 1997 when several critics of the leadership were replaced by people who were loyal to Tony Blair (see Chapter Two). The party's Assistant General Secretary, Tommy Sheppard, was another casualty of reform and later published his own plans for the restructuring of the party north of the border, including proposals that there should be Scottish control of party membership and finance, that the party leader in

Scotland should be elected by the membership, and that there should be greater autonomy over policy in Scotland. In many respects, and despite its electoral strength, Labour faces the most serious challenge of all the parties in Scotland: who makes policy – London or Edinburgh? The establishment of a new so-called Blairite group, initially named The Network and later known as Scottish Labour Forum (SLF), added to speculation about potential divisions between Old and New Labour in Scotland. In March 1998, Scottish Labour Action (SLA) agreed to wind-up the group following consultation with its members. The SLA was established in the 1980s in order to focus on and develop plans for home rule, and its demise has added to speculation about the realignment of political forces within the Scottish Labour Party, as well as on the Left more generally.

The Labour Party in Scotland agreed several proposals for change at its conference in March 1998. In future the conference would no longer debate motions and composite motions as in the past. Instead Policy Forums would have responsibility for policy-making. The Scottish executive would be reduced in size, and the post of General Secretary of the Scottish party would be altered in recognition that a Scottish leader in the new Parliament would take on a new role in Scotland. The manifesto for the Scottish Parliament elections would, however, be drawn up in Scotland. In respect of candidates for the Scottish Parliament, the party introduced major changes. A panel of 20 members (five national executive committee, five Scottish executive committee, five Labour Party members and five Independents) were given the task of considering written applications from prospective candidates, selecting those who would move to interview at the next stage of the process, and then compiling a panel of prospective candidates from which local constituencies could chose. There was much suspicion of this process and speculation that the panel was operating an 'ideological' test excluding those who have expressed dissent in the past. The Scottish Secretary, Donald Dewar, vigorously defended the reforms and the selection process on the grounds that it was crucial for the party to select the best and most talented people to represent it in the new Parliament.

As a party committed to UK federalism, the Scottish Liberal Democrats did not face the same kind of pressures as both the

Conservative and Labour Parties in Scotland (Lynch, 1998). The questions for them surround political strategy and possible coalitions with other parties. Given their association in the Scottish Constitutional Convention, the Scottish Liberal Democrats are seen as the most likely coalition partners for the Scottish Labour Party, although the SNP also consider them possible coalition allies.

The Scottish National Party can be seen as the most likely beneficiaries of a Scottish Parliament. As the self-evidently 'Scottish' party, they are in a position to maximise their vote in a Scottish Parliament. However, home rule is a means not an end for the Nationalists, who see it as a stepping-stone to full independence. Fundamentalist critics within the party are less sanguine than the leadership that this can be made to work. Their former MP Margo MacDonald has counselled against what she sees as the 'devolution swamp'. The related difficulty for the SNP is how to evolve distinctive policy agendas in Scotland when the Parliament does not have a full range of constitutional powers.

New Politics?

The quest for a Scottish Parliament had not been that of Scotland's non-Conservative parties alone. Indeed, as we will see in the next chapter, it can be argued that, from the late 1980s when the Scottish Constitutional Convention was formed, they played a fairly minor role, and that it was associations of civic society which made the running. Many organisations and groups in Scottish society have become accustomed to playing their part in developing the proposals for change. To take one example: the demand for equal representation for women in a Scottish Parliament did not come about primarily because the political parties wanted it, but because a broad coalition of women's groups focused their campaign on this issue, and the parties had to accede to this if they were to retain women's votes (Brown, 1996). As the plans for the Parliament are evolving, different institutions throughout Scotland are considering how they can continue to influence the debate and to be involved in power-sharing in the new legislature. Wider civil society will seek to continue to influence the agenda by using different avenues and channels for participation. One possibility is a continued role for the Scottish

Civic Assembly, which groups together a variety of civic pressure groups and aspires to be a sort of civil-society guardian of the ideals which emerged in and around the Constitutional Convention.

Designing new procedures and Parliamentary arrangements are seen as another approach to ensure that power does not reside exclusively with the executive. The operation and role of Parliamentary committees is viewed in particular as an important forum in which Scottish society can be involved in key decisions, especially if the committees have the power to initiate as well as scrutinise and monitor the effects of proposed legislation.

The work of the Consultative Steering Group set up by the Secretary of State in January 1998 may prove to be important in this regard because it includes not just representatives from the four main parties in Scotland, but also people nominated by the Scottish Constitutional Convention and the Convention of Scottish Local Authorities and others representing different interests from the trade union movement, the business sector, consumers and equal opportunities. Their remit is to gather evidence from expert panels and to put forward recommendations for standing orders based on a number of principles. These principles include the sharing of power, accountability, accessibility, openness and responsiveness, and equal opportunities. As part of the process the government has announced a wide consultation with over 800 organisations in Scotland and has invited individuals also to submit their views and ideas on different aspects of Parliamentary arrangements. In addition, examples of good practice and experiences in other countries are being considered.

It is hard to predict the outcome of the process. Nevertheless, there is a possibility that in several respects the standing orders and procedures for the Scottish Parliament will differ substantially from the Westminster model, and that the balance of power among the parties and between the people and the Scottish Parliament will be different. However, this prediction has to be set against the inherent conservatism of party politics in Scotland.

CONCLUSION

At the time of writing, we can only speculate about the potential impact of a new institution, the Scottish Parliament, on party politics in Scotland. The establishment of a new legislature will bring a whole range of domestic policies under democratic control. However, the fact that it will be only a home rule Parliament means that what happens in the wider British political arena will continue to have an important influence on Scottish affairs.

The creation of a new Parliament after nearly 300 years has meant that much of the focus has been on its relationship with the Westminster one which has retained theoretical sovereignty over the Scottish Parliament. While focusing on this relationship between the two Parliaments is right and proper, it ignores a key dimension, namely how a Scottish Parliament will relate to its own civil society (Paterson, 1998a). To put it simply, who will be the creature of whom? Will the political institution assume primacy in speaking for Scotland? Or will Scottish civil society, which has played a prominent role in creating and shaping that Parliament, assume that it and 'the people' are paramount? There is a sufficient history in Scotland of tensions over where sovereignty resides – in the 'Crown', the Parliament, or the people – to make this a live and ongoing debate. It also touches on the key question of the purposes of that Parliament. To put it another way: it is not simply what the Parliament will do and what its functions are, but what it is for – that is, what it will achieve in and for the wider society.

There is a tendency in much political writing to focus on the institutions of government, on how Parliaments function and operate as relatively autonomous systems, and on what we might call the 'supply' side of the political system. In this book – which is, after all, about the Scottish *electorate* – we want to redress that balance to focus on the 'demand' side – what people want from political institutions. How different is the Scottish electorate from the wider British one? What lies behind the divergence in voting behaviours north and south of the border over the last 25 years? Can we identify different values and preferences in Scotland?

The existence of a Scottish Parliament will change substantially the political context in which party politics are played out, as well as providing a new political agenda within which Scottish politics takes place. In this chapter we have discussed the possible effects on the distribution of seats between the parties in adopting the Additional

Member System for the elections. We have also considered the influence of the setting up of the new Parliament on the internal relationships of the political parties and their possible relationships with each other. And we have discussed the potential for sharing of power and greater pluralism within the political system in Scotland in the future.

Some of the answers to the questions we have posed will be evident following the elections in May 1999. In previous general elections, the key question in Scotland has been 'Who speaks for Scotland?' (Brown, 1997). Within a Westminster system, where the SNP are unable to form a government, over 45 per cent of the electorate voted for the Labour Party as the party most likely to defeat the Conservatives and to deliver constitutional change. In a Scottish Parliament, it can be argued, there is much more point in voting SNP, either to put pressure on Labour to deliver the type of policies Scotland wants or to be elected in their own right. As some commentators have put it, there is every reason for the SNP to feel confident as they will be playing on their own ground. 'Who speaks for Scotland in Scotland?' is thus a more difficult question to answer. From the evidence so far, there is support for the view expressed by Dunleavy et al (1997) that 'Scotland's already well-established political distinctiveness will continue to develop as the first Scottish Parliament is elected and begins its proceedings'.

2

The 1997 General Election: Background, Campaign, Results, Consequences

INTRODUCTION

The morning after the 1997 general election in Scotland stands in sharp contrast to that following the election in 1992. After a campaign that seemed to have lasted for the intervening five years, people in Scotland woke up to the news not just of a Labour victory and a record majority in the House of Commons, but to the fact that not one candidate from the Conservative Party had been elected to represent a Scottish constituency. While a Tory wipe-out was predicted by a few more foolhardy commentators in 1992, no such speculation was being made in 1997 in spite of evidence from the opinion polls showing the Conservatives in a very weak position and the fact that the party had performed badly in the European and local elections in 1995. Indeed there was a cautious air about the pre-election predictions in Scotland. The memory of 1992, when the Conservatives actually increased their percentage vote and number of seats in Scotland, still haunted those who had looked forward to a change of government. The reason for this caution can be explained partly by the central role of the constitutional question in Scottish politics and by the belief that so much was at stake. For political opponents of the Conservatives, the object was not just to replace the government but to have an opportunity to fulfil some of the hopes and aspirations for home rule in Scotland.

This chapter outlines the background to the election campaign before assessing the results of the election and the consequences for Scottish and British politics. In Chapter One we identified four key dates in Scottish political history prior to 1997, namely 1832, 1886, 1922 and 1974. Similarly, we can highlight three key general elections in the post-war period:

- The election of the Labour government in 1945 committed to developing and expanding the welfare state and to combating unemployment through the use of Keynesian demand management.
- The return of a Labour government in 1964 after thirteen years of Conservative rule on a platform of major social reforms.
- The election of the first Thatcher government in 1979 promising a radical break with the politics of the so-called post-war consensus and offering a future based on monetarism, the rolling back of the state and the adherence to free market principles.

The general election of 1997 promises to go down in history on several grounds, not least because of the number of records broken (Norris, 1997), but also because of the new Labour government's programme of constitutional change. In the first session of Parliament the government outlined its plans to hold referendums on devolution in Scotland and Wales, to hold a referendum on the establishment of a strategic authority for London including the election of a mayor, and to set up regional development agencies in England. Plans for introducing proportional representation for elections to the European Parliament were announced, and a freedom of information White Paper was published. Other proposals for reforming the House of Lords and introducing electoral reform for the House of Commons are being considered. As we discuss below, constitutional change for Scotland could have far-reaching implications for reform in other parts of the UK, especially within the context of political developments in Northern Ireland and the wider context of the process of broadening and deepening the European Union.

POLITICAL DEVELOPMENTS IN SCOTLAND AFTER 1992

For supporters of constitutional change the results of the 1992 general election and the return of the Conservative government were a significant setback. James Mitchell (1992) argues that it had the same impact as the referendum of 1979 in that 'though a numeric majority voted for change, the failure to realise expectations was a psychological blow to the opposition parties'. The immediate reaction of the opposition was not edifying as they sought to find an explanation for the result (MacWhirter, 1992). Initial efforts to bring the opposition parties together were made by Campbell Christie, the General Secretary of the Scottish Trades Union Congress and key player in the Scottish Constitutional Convention, but they failed. A mood of depression engulfed the Scottish Labour Party, while the leader of the Scottish Liberal Democrats, Malcolm Bruce, argued that their stance on devolution and their involvement in the Scottish Constitutional Convention had been electorally damaging. The Scottish National Party referred back to their pre-election warning that the Labour Party could not win the general election and that supporters of constitutional change had no alternative but to vote for the SNP. In contrast, members of the Conservative Party who had expected at least some losses in the general election were perhaps the most surprised of all to have witnessed a marginal increase in electoral support from 24 per cent to 25.7 per cent and the return of 11 MPs to Westminster, one more than in 1992. Although the Conservative Party enjoyed this modest recovery, the claim was reiterated that the majority of Scots still voted for parties which were in favour of constitutional change, and reference was made again to the 'democratic deficit' in Scotland on the grounds that the Conservative Party had no mandate to rule in Scotland.

In recognition that the demand for constitutional change had not evaporated with their return to office, the Conservative Party announced minor constitutional changes following its 'taking stock' exercise, including the decision in 1995 to hold meetings of the Scottish Grand Committee in different venues throughout Scotland. However, for their political opponents such measures were no more than a cosmetic exercise, although the meetings of the Grand

Committee were used, particularly by pressure groups, as a way of lobbying and protesting about government policy in Scotland.

Campaign Groups

The immediate post-election period witnessed the setting up of several organisations which had the aim of keeping the constitutional question high on the political agenda. Democracy for Scotland, Scotland United and Common Cause were three such bodies and the Women's Co-ordination Group was also established to continue pressing the case for equal representation of men and women in a Scottish Parliament. Although the different groups continued to exist, an umbrella organisation, the Coalition for Scottish Democracy, was established in 1995 and was instrumental in setting up a Scottish Civic Assembly. The Assembly had representatives from a wide range of non-party organisations in Scotland and played a role in articulating an alternative to the government's approach to policy issues in Scotland.

Despite predictions to the contrary, the Scottish Constitutional Convention also survived and set up a Scottish Constitutional Commission to take forward the Convention's scheme (Lynch, 1996b). A certain urgency pervaded the work of the Convention, and the desire was to have an agreed scheme in place in time to influence events at the next general election. This sense of urgency was precipitated by the view that the Prime Minister, John Major, was vulnerable in the wake of the financial crisis that followed the events of Black Wednesday in September 1992 (Gavin and Sanders, 1997), and continued as pressure on the government built up over the following years. The launching of the Scottish Constitutional Convention's final document, *Scotland's Parliament, Scotland's Right*, on St Andrew's Day in November 1995 was significant not only because it represented a consensus of view between two of Scotland's main political parties and among a wide range of organisations in Scottish civil society on a scheme for a Scottish Parliament, but because of the reaction it provoked from the Prime Minister. Accusing the members of the Convention of indulging in 'teenage madness' (a strange description given the average age of Convention activists), and warning of the break-up of the United Kingdom, John Major believed that he could build on the opposition to constitutional change which he believed had won the election in 1992 for the Conservatives.

The Convention proposed a Scottish Parliament of 129 members to be elected by a version of the Additional Member System (see Chapter One). Parties in the Convention also signed an Electoral Agreement in which they committed themselves to the principle of equal representation in the first Parliament and to field an equal number of men and women in winnable seats in order to achieve this aim (Brown, 1996). The Convention's document outlined the powers and functions of a Scottish Parliament, including what turned out to be the most controversial aspect of the scheme, the power to vary the basic rate of income tax by a maximum of three pence in the pound (SCC, 1995).

Elections

While the campaign for constitutional change continued, key elections in the post-1992 period were also significant and provided some evidence of the change that was about to occur in 1997. By-elections were called as a result of the death of two MPs, John Smith in 1994 and Nicholas Fairbairn in 1995. The death of John Smith, the Labour leader, came as an enormous blow to the campaigners for change, for personal and political reasons. In addition to his qualities as leader of the Labour Party, John Smith was viewed as a guardian of the constitutional question, having been Michael Foot's deputy in piloting the Scotland Bill through the House of Commons in the 1970s, and was trusted to work effectively towards the establishment of a Scottish Parliament and to complete what he described as 'unfinished business'. The by-election that followed in Monklands East was held in the context of accusations of religious sectarianism and provided another opportunity for intense partisan conflict between the Labour Party and the SNP. The seat was won by Helen Liddell, former general secretary of the Labour Party in Scotland, although the SNP came close. They were rewarded in a second by-election the following year when they took Perth and Kinross from the Conservatives. The election of Roseanna Cunningham for the SNP – a nationalist, republican, socialist, feminist – in place of one of

Scotland's more traditional and flamboyant Conservative MPs did not go unnoticed by commentators.

The period also witnessed four other elections, the District elections which quickly followed the 1992 general election, the Regional and European elections in 1994 and the elections for the shadow unitary local authorities in 1995. Before the 1994 European election, Labour held seven of Scotland's eight European constituencies, with the SNP holding one seat. While Labour retained six of its seats at the election with 42.5 per cent of the vote, the SNP was successful in winning North East Scotland from Labour and in achieving 32.6 per cent of the vote across Scotland, an increase of seven per cent on the 1989 European election results. The Conservatives lost support in every Euro-constituency in Scotland and experienced a decline of 6.4 per cent of their overall electoral support (Denver, 1994).

The elections for the shadow unitary authorities in 1995 followed a major restructuring of local government in Scotland. The decision to move from a two-tier local government system of nine Regions, 53 Districts and three Island authorities to a unitary system of 29 new authorities on the mainland along with the three Island authorities was taken following limited consultation and in the absence of a Commission to examine the proposals for change (McCrone et al, 1993). Ian Lang (1994a), the then Secretary of State for Scotland, answered the criticism that the case for reform had not been made by citing the benefits of a single-tier structure as efficiency, effectiveness and an improvement in local democracy and involvement. The government was also accused of gerrymandering the boundaries of the new authorities in an attempt to gain political advantage. If this was the intention then it failed miserably, as the election results can only be interpreted as a catastrophe for the Conservatives (Denver and Bochel, 1995). The Conservatives' share of the votes dropped to 11.3 per cent leaving the government without control of any of Scotland's local authorities. This gave support to the view that the party did not have a mandate to rule in Scotland and that the democratic deficit was exacerbated. In contrast, Labour reasserted its dominance of Scottish local government winning control of 20 of the 29 new authorities. In hindsight it can be seen that both the European and the local elections helped pave the way for the defeat of the Conservatives on 1 May 1997. As Philip Norton (1997) observed, although the writing was on the wall for the Conservatives, the problem was that they had forgotten how to read.

THE LONG CAMPAIGN

As pressure on the government mounted and their majority in the House of Commons was depleted, the political parties in Scotland prepared for the general election. The Scottish Labour Party and the Scottish Liberal Democrats consolidated and articulated their support for the home rule scheme agreed in the Scottish Constitutional Convention, and the SNP put forward their own detailed proposals for 'independence in Europe' and for a 200-member Scottish Parliament elected by a Single Transferable Vote electoral system. Meanwhile the Conservative Party in Scotland, under the leadership of the new Secretary of State, Michael Forsyth, began a concerted campaign against the Convention's scheme, especially the decision to give the Scottish Parliament tax-varying powers. Although Iain MacWhirter (1995) likened the appointment of Michael Forsyth to the post to 'trying to put out a house fire by throwing petrol over it', the new Minister was true to form in his political opposition to this particular proposal, dubbing it the 'Tartan Tax' (Forsyth, 1995). The effectiveness of this attack on the Labour Party in particular was to be demonstrated by events that followed.

Attempts by the Scottish Labour Party to gain more autonomy of decision-making were affected by the election of the new leader, Tony Blair, and the injection of 'New Labour' policies and ideas north of the border. Political differences were evident over controversial issues such as the reform of Clause IV of the party's constitution (on nationalisation) and other aspects of policy such as education, and most crucially taxation and spending. To the surprise of many – not least members of the party in Scotland and their Convention partners, the Scottish Liberal Democrats – the Labour Party also announced its plans to hold a two-question referendum on the constitutional question.

Before the announcement was made, the line of argument advanced by the Scottish Labour Party and by its leader, George Robertson, was that the mandate for constitutional change had already been given by the fact that around 75 per cent of the Scottish electorate consistently voted for parties which supported reform. The party argued that it was a sufficient mandate that Labour should win a general election on a platform that included plans to set up a Scottish Parliament. In these circumstances, the reaction from political activists to the party leadership's decision to hold a referendum on the issue was somewhat predictable. Labour was accused of once again betraying the hopes and aspirations of Scots for home rule and Scottish Labour was criticised for being under the control of the leader, Tony Blair. It was interesting to compare the response of the media and commentators north and south of the border to the change of policy. For those in England, the decision seemed politically sensible and a way of endorsing and strengthening the plans for a Scottish Parliament. In Scotland, on the other hand, the initial reaction was to interpret the decision as potential political suicide, leaving Labour open to losing electoral ground to the SNP, and one that could seriously endanger the setting up of a Parliament. To understand the mood that followed the decision to hold a referendum in Scotland, it has to be placed in the context of memories of the referendum experience in the 1970s. For those who had been part of the 'Yes' campaign in 1979, it was interpreted as another obstacle in the long road to home rule and anxieties were raised that history would repeat itself especially if the referendum was subject to a 40 per cent rule or other condition (Jones, 1997).

The debate became more heated when it was announced that there were going to be two questions, the first asking people in Scotland if they wanted a Scottish Parliament and the second directed at the tax-varying powers. The split over the decision to hold a referendum was rehearsed at executive meetings of the Scottish Labour Party where attempts were made to limit the damage by restricting it to a straightforward question on whether or not to establish a Parliament. At one stage, following a particularly difficult executive meeting, a so-called compromise of three questions was proposed, a decision that only added fuel to the debate. In the event, a final decision was made for a two-question referendum – one on the Parliament and one on the tax question – and Tony Blair arrived in Scotland to explain why the decision had been taken, at one stage saying that it had originated from a proposal from his Shadow Secretary of State for Scotland, George Robertson. The argument was made that, without a referendum, the plans for a Parliament were open to attack from supporters of the status quo; this would be a particular danger, it was claimed, especially for the decision over tax-raising powers that had already been the subject of attack from Michael Forsyth and others. The latter point was, of course, related very directly to the Labour Party's policy on taxation and its determination to rid itself of the image of a tax-raising party. The argument was also put by the Labour leadership that a 'Yes' vote in the referendum would ease the passage of a Scotland Bill through the House of Commons and help entrench the Scottish Parliament and make it less vulnerable in the future should the Conservatives return to power at Westminster.

The SNP, not surprisingly, jumped at the opportunity handed to it to make political capital from the decision, accusing George Robertson of being a puppet of Tony Blair and stating that once again policy in Scotland was being driven from south of the border. Tony Blair was even compared by some to Margaret Thatcher in that he was accused of being insensitive to the political situation in Scotland. The storm mounted as the SNP got hold of a research report based on evidence from focus groups, carried out on behalf of the Scottish Labour Party, which showed that Blair was identified with moving Labour to the right and that Labour was seen to be back-tracking on the commitment to home rule (Jones, 1997). The Scottish Liberal Democrats reiterated their strong opposition to the holding of a referendum on the grounds that the mandate for such constitutional change had already been demonstrated by the Scottish electorate. They were particularly opposed to the second question on taxation fearing that a Parliament without the ability to raise revenue would not have the type of powers envisaged in the plans of the Scottish Constitutional Convention.

Those within the Scottish Labour Party who opposed the referendum decision found their positions under threat as the party moved closer to the general election and demonstrated its willingness to impose party discipline. Suspicions within the party mounted and were fuelled by the news that a group of senior Labour activists broadly sympathetic to Tony Blair and the policies of New Labour has formed a group called The Network (*The Scotsman*, 29 January 1997). At the elections for the Scottish executive which followed in March 1997, a number of well-known members on the left lost their positions, reflecting the change in the balance of power in the party in Scotland

These developments meant that many Labour activists in Scotland entered the official campaign with very mixed feelings. They desperately wanted a change of government, but the shift away from the type of policies they supported and the referendum issue severely damaged morale. However, with an election imminent, the majority view was that there was little option but to accept the decisions and move into the campaign. While some of the party's supporters were disillusioned, if the object was to get a change of government, then the Labour Party was the only means to achieve it.

It was not only the Scottish Labour Party that was facing difficulties. The Scottish Conservative and Unionist Party encountered its own problems following the sudden resignation of Allan Stewart, sitting MP for Eastwood, in the spring of 1997. Sir Michael Hirst, tipped as a possible successor to Stewart, caused further confusion when he dramatically withdrew his candidacy and resigned as chair of the party. The latter event was precipitated by threats made by political opponents within the party to reveal evidence about Michael Hirst's private life. The disarray and divisions within the party were also exposed in their response to the constitutional question. While the Health Secretary, Stephen Dorrell, warned that a future Tory government would abolish a Scottish Parliament should it be established, the Secretary of State for Scotland, Michael Forsyth, repeated his view that a Scottish Parliament which had the endorsement of the people of Scotland would not be abolished easily: 'a Scottish Parliament is not just for Christmas, it's for life' (*The Scotsman*, 11 February 1997).

Given the criticism of the accuracy of opinion polls in predicting the outcome of the 1992 general election, the evidence from the polls in the run-up to the 1997 election was treated with some caution. Learning from the 1992 experience, the pollsters had changed their methods. In fact, the opinion polls got the election result more or less correct, at least compared with 1992. Evidence of what was to come was available in a February poll in which nearly three-quarters of respondents in Scotland viewed the Conservatives as an 'English party with little relevance to Scotland'. Polls conducted by ICM throughout the election campaign estimated Labour's vote in Scotland at under 50 per cent and the poll conducted just two days before the election came within one percentage point of the Scottish result. The poll indicated that there was virtually no gender gap in the voting intentions of men and women, with the exception of a split in the male/female support for the Liberal Democrats. Polls conducted by System Three had recorded a reasonably consistent pattern of support for constitutional change with 40 per cent of potential voters supporting the home rule option and 30 per cent preferring independence, leaving just 20 per cent in favour of the status quo. Asked about how they would vote on a two-question referendum for a Scottish Parliament, 69 per cent of respondents to the ICM poll in January said they wanted a Scottish Parliament within the UK and 59 per cent also agreed with the statement that a devolved Parliament should have the power to vary income tax by up to three pence in the pound (*The Scotsman*, 22 January 1997). Testing the opinion of voters outside Scotland on constitutional change, ICM conducted a poll of a representative sample of people across Britain (*The Scotsman*, 28 January 1997). Almost 50 per cent of those polled supported constitutional change, 15 per cent preferring independence in Europe for Scotland and 33 per cent devolution within the UK. A minority, 38 per cent, noted their preference for the status quo. The evidence from this poll gave little credence to the Conservative government's claim that there was strong opposition in England to the establishment of a Scottish Parliament.

When the decision was finally announced in March to hold the election in May 1997, there was enormous relief that the long wait would soon be over. The main activity in the campaign was concentrated in key marginals, and surprisingly a number of the issues remained remarkably absent from the debates. Unlike the campaign in England, the European question did not have the same impact in Scotland. Instead the constitutional question dominated the media coverage. Again Tony Blair hit the headlines in an interview with a journalist from *The Scotsman* newspaper when he remarked that, even with the establishment of a Scottish Parliament, 'sovereignty rests with me as an English MP and that's the way it will stay'. Responding to questions on the Scottish Parliament's ability to raise tax, the Labour leader was accused of comparing a Parliament in Scotland to a 'parish council' in England, even though he was trying to make the perfectly reasonable point that even the smallest English parish council had the right to levy taxes so why should such a power be denied to the Scottish Parliament. Nevertheless, the comment was seized upon by critics as proof that Blair only wanted Scotland to have a parish council equivalent.

One of the key issues in Scottish politics is 'who speaks for Scotland?' by which is meant which of the parties can be most trusted to represent Scottish interests in Westminster (Brown et al, 1998). In the run-up to the election, the SNP leader, Alex Salmond, made much of Tony Blair's comments on a Parliament, accusing Labour of being a single issue party 'that issue being the pursuit of power by Tony Blair in Middle England, regardless of what Scotland needs and wants'. Blair responded by stating that Scotland itself was at the heart of the concerns of people in Scotland, and argued that one question summed it up the issue at the election: 'who will speak for Scotland?' (*The Herald*, 30 April 1997). On election day itself, as the discussion of the results below demonstrates, another key question appears to have exercised most voters' minds and that was 'which party is most likely to defeat the Conservatives?'.

One of the surprising features of the campaign was the low profile played by the Conservative Party and some of its leaders such as Michael Forsyth. The Labour Party expected the attack on the constitutional question and the 'Tartan Tax' to continue, and although John Major could be relied upon to make speeches warning against the break-up of the United Kingdom and the 'slippery slope' to independence if Scotland went down the home rule road, the Secretary of State for Scotland was often conspicuous by his absence. Could it be that the 'Tartan Tax' campaign had peaked too early, or that Tony Blair had adopted the correct political tactics by deciding to hold a referendum? The weekend before the election, the front page of *Scotland on Sunday* featured Michael Forsyth (Secretary of State), Malcolm Rifkind (Foreign Secretary) and Ian Lang (Trade Secretary) with the headline 'Yesterday's Men'. They publicised the results of an

ICM poll which predicted that all three would lose their seats in Stirling, Edinburgh Pentlands and Galloway and Upper Nithsdale respectively, the first two to Labour and the third to the SNP (*Scotland on Sunday*, 27 April 1997).

There was little comfort also for the Conservatives from the business community. Although some companies had come out strongly against a Parliament in 1992, threatening to pull out of Scotland if Labour won the election, few views of this nature were being articulated publicly in 1997. The exception was some controversial remarks made by the Governor of the Bank of Scotland. Some attempts were made to highlight the potential negative effects of levying higher taxes in Scotland, with evidence for and against being advanced by different accountancy experts. Moreover, Michael Forsyth's last-minute claim that the Treasury would use the opportunity of constitutional change to slash Scotland's budget by £2.5bn met with little support (*The Herald*, 30 April 1997). It seemed that, if the government had failed to spot the warning signs, the business community was much more adept at reading the writing on the wall and so kept a low profile during the campaign.

THE RESULTS

The results confirmed that writing. At the 1992 general election, Labour had won 49 seats with 39 per cent of the vote, the Conservatives 11 seats with 25.7 per cent, the Liberal Democrats returned nine with 13.1 per cent and the SNP just three with 21.5 per cent of the vote (Bochel and Denver, 1992). On 1 May 1997 history was made when, in spite of receiving 17.5 per cent of the vote, the Conservatives lost all their seats in Scotland, including their stronghold of Eastwood. Labour again benefited from the first-past-the post system by achieving 56 seats with 45.6 per cent of the vote, followed by the Liberal Democrats with ten seats and 13 per cent of the vote and the SNP with six seats and 22.1 per cent of the vote (see Tables 2.1 and 2.2). Journalists in Scotland searched for words adequate to describe what had happened.

Party fortunes clearly varied significantly, with an 8.2 per cent reduction in support for the Conservatives as against a 6.6 per cent increase in the votes for the Labour Party. Labour gained Aberdeen

South, Ayr, Eastwood, Edinburgh Pentlands, Dumfries and Stirling, and was also successful in winning the four-way marginal in Inverness East, Nairn and Lochaber. The percentage of the votes for the Scottish Liberal Democrats was almost static but, because of its distribution, had the result of increasing the party's seats from nine to ten. They were successful in holding on to Gordon in spite of the boundary changes that made it vulnerable to a challenge from the Conservatives, and they held Tweeddale, Ettrick and Lauderdale following the retiral of Sir David Steel. The party also gained two seats from the Conservatives, Edinburgh West and West Aberdeenshire and Kincardine. Votes for the SNP increased modestly by just 0.6 per cent, while their seats doubled from three to six, as they retained Perth and Kinross and won Tayside North and Galloway and Upper Nithsdale from the Conservatives. However, the SNP failed to win Glasgow Govan: Mohammed Sarwar was elected to represent Labour and held off strong opposition from the SNP candidate, Nicola Sturgeon. This was a disappointing result for the party which hoped to mount a greater challenge to Labour's dominance of seats in Scotland. The first-past-the-post electoral system very much worked against the SNP and the relatively even spread of their vote across the country. This can be contrasted with the concentration of support for the Liberal Democrats and their success in terms of seats with a lower percentage of the vote.

Table 2.1:   Percentage share of the vote in Scotland, 1992-1997

	1992	1997	Change
Conservative	25.7	17.5	-8.2%
Labour	39.0	45.6	+6.6%
Liberal Democrat	13.1	13.0	-0.1%
SNP	21.5	22.1	+0.6%
Others	0.8	1.9	+1.1%

Table 2.2: The distribution of seats in Scotland, 1992-1997

	1992	1997	Change
Conservative	11	0	-11
Labour	49	56	+7
Liberal Democrat	9	10	+1
SNP	3	6	+3
Others	0	0	0

The turnout of electors dropped in Scotland from an average of 75.4 per cent in 1992 to 71.4 per cent in 1997, although the drop was smaller than in Britain as a whole (Denver, 1997). Changes in support for the four main political parties varied in different parts of Scotland and reflected the willingness of the electorate to vote tactically, most obviously by voting for the party most likely to defeat the Conservatives. As a result, Conservative support fell more heavily in the seats they were defending. In a four-party system, it is difficult to make direct comparison with the results of the election in England. For example, although the swing against the Conservatives was an average of 10.5 per cent across the whole of Great Britain, it was just 7.5 per cent in Scotland. The difference in the swing has to be analysed within the context of Labour's dominant position in Scottish politics and the fact that it is operating in a four-party system, and also in the context of a longer history of anti-Conservative tactical voting in Scotland: for example, the party had lost 11 of their then 21 seats at the 1987 general election. A similar situation exists in Wales where the swing was 7.4 per cent against the Conservatives, enough to result in a wipe-out for the party in both countries.

Eighteen new MPs were elected to represent Scottish constituencies, including 14 from the Labour Party. The gender balance of MPs also altered significantly, with the increase in the number of women MPs from five in 1992 to 12 in 1997, a rise in the representation rate from 6.9 per cent to 16.6 per cent. The impact of

Labour's policy of all-women shortlists in 50 per cent of its winnable and vacant seats was reflected in the fact that nine of the women MPs were elected to represent the Labour Party, with just one from the Liberal Democrats; the SNP had two. The new Labour government at Westminster also reflects the influence of Scottish MPs, with several holding key ministerial posts, prompting some commentators to remark on what they perceive to be an over-representation of Scottish interests. Events that followed the general election added to this perception.

THE CONSEQUENCES

The longer term effect of 1 May will take some time to absorb and assess, but the impact on the Conservative Party in Scotland was immediately felt as the party struggled to come to terms with their wipe-out. The new government lost little time in moving to implement its manifesto commitments. The new Prime Minister, Tony Blair, dropped George Robertson as the Secretary of State for Scotland in favour of Donald Dewar, MP for Anniesland. He was supported by a Scottish Office ministerial team of Malcolm Chisholm, Sam Galbraith, Henry McLeish, Brian Wilson (in the Commons) and John Sewell in the Lords. Those involved in the campaign for a Scottish Parliament were also anxious to register their support for a double 'Yes' vote in the proposed referendum. They reacted immediately to Labour's victory by putting into place an umbrella organisation, Partnership for a Parliament, which in turn made plans to launch the referendum campaign under the organisation Scotland Forward. In anticipation of the election result, funding for the campaign had been raised mainly from the trade unions and largely at the instigation of a pro-home rule businessman, Nigel Smith, a long-term supporter of constitutional change. The campaign was formally launched on 15 May 1997, the same day as the government introduced its Referendum Bill to the House of Commons.

The Minister of State at the Scottish Office responsible for overseeing the home rule plans, Henry McLeish, gave his assurance that Labour would move quickly in proceeding with a referendum. The holding of the referendum in the early days of the government can be contrasted with the experience in the 1970s, when it was held after the government had been in office for five years. Henry McLeish was also present to launch the campaign on behalf of women activists in Scotland organised by the Scottish Women's Co-ordination Group on 7 June, in his capacity not only as Minister with responsibility for devolution but also as the Minister in the Scottish Office responsible for women's issues. He used this opportunity to reinforce the government's commitment to change, stating that the Referendum Bill was 'the first Bill to be published, the first Bill to have a second reading and the first Bill to go through the House of Commons'. The government faced some criticism from opponents, however, for subjecting the passage of the Bill to a guillotine motion in the House of Commons, and for noting its intention to hold a referendum on the basis of a White Paper rather than an actual Scotland Bill. Unsuccessful attempts were made at the next stage, the introduction of the Referendum Bill into the House of Lords, to knock the government off course. Given the size of the government's majority, this was never a serious proposition, and the government kept to its timetable by publishing its White Paper on a Scottish Parliament in July 1997. To the surprise of many, not least the government, the White Paper became a best-seller, selling over 25,000 copies. The referendum in Scotland was set for 11 September 1997 with two questions to be asked: 'I agree/do not agree that there should be a Scottish Parliament'; and 'I agree/do not agree that a Scottish Parliament should have tax-varying powers'.

Labour's partners in the Scottish Constitutional Convention, the Scottish Liberal Democrats, put aside their opposition to the referendum and joined the broad-based campaign for the double 'Yes' vote (as it was usually called, despite the wording of the questions). The campaign was strengthened considerably by the involvement of the SNP. Although fundamentalists in the party maintained their opposition, claiming that the party stood for independence not devolution, the party leader, Alex Salmond, made it clear that he would support a 'positive' White Paper. In early August, the party's national council voted to support the Yes/Yes campaign. Labour and Liberal Democrats welcomed this conversion, although a few Labour activists with long memories of 1979 refused to associate themselves with what they saw as an SNP attempt to use the Parliament as a route to full independence.

As the campaign gathered force, what was less easy to identify was a credible opposition campaign. This was in marked contrast to the 1970s when the 'No' campaign was well financed and organised and the 'Yes' campaign was poorly funded and divided. The Think Twice campaign took time to respond and, following their resounding defeat at the general election, the Conservative Party in Scotland appeared to have little energy left to mount a significant or united attack on Labour's proposals. Moreover, early opinion polls were showing substantial leads on both questions: three to one on the principle of a Scottish Parliament, and two to one in favour of its having tax-varying powers.

All campaign activity was suspended for one week in early September following the unexpected death of Princess Diana. Home rule campaigners speculated on the potential negative impact of the event on the referendum result. Their fears were unfounded. On a turnout of 60.4 per cent, a respectable percentage given that the electoral roll was out-of-date, over 74 per cent voted in favour on the first question, and more than 63 per cent on the second. All regions in Scotland voted in favour on the first question, and all but two also did so on the second: Orkney had 52.6 per cent opposed to the tax powers, and Dumfries and Galloway had 51.2 per cent opposed. With hindsight, it appeared that the people of Scotland had made up their mind on the constitutional question long before the campaign for change had begun. With such strong support in the referendum, the 'unfinished business' which the late Labour leader John Smith had spoken of in the context of home rule was settled. Scotland would have a Scottish Parliament. The Scotland Bill was drafted and published before the end of the year. The Bill entered the House of Commons in January 1998 and the political parties began the process of selecting their candidates for the elections in May 1999.

CONCLUSION

In Scotland, the 1997 general election will be remembered particularly because of the wipe-out of the Conservative Party and the introduction of major constitutional change, paving the way for a Scottish

Parliament. While the results across Britain as a whole showed a slight narrowing of the north/south divide in support for the Labour and Conservative Parties, the constitutional debate in Scotland and the four-party system mean that politics in Scotland continue to be different from other parts of Britain. The establishment of a Scottish Parliament will add to its distinctive character.

The remainder of this book looks in more depth at why the election results turned out as they did, at why the referendum produced such an emphatic endorsement of home rule, and at the prospects for Scottish politics as the new Parliament is established.

3

Social Structure, Identity and Voting Behaviour

INTRODUCTION

In Chapters One and Two we outlined the background to the 1997 general election in Scotland. In this chapter we present the first of our results from the 1997 Scottish Election Survey, a nationally representative survey of 852 members of the Scottish electorate. (Further details of the survey are in the Appendix.) We begin by looking at how the behaviour and attitudes of the electorate in Scotland changed between the 1992 and 1997 general elections; we then go on to look at the reasons people in Scotland gave for their vote at the 1997 general election. In the second part of the chapter we focus on sociological explanations of voting behaviour (Barry, 1970). We focus first on the social structure of Scotland, to assess the extent to which voting behaviour in Scotland is explicable in terms of social location. In this section we look at the impact of a range of indicators of social location to assess their impact on voting behaviour. Second, we examine the contribution of identity to voting behaviour. In this section we are concerned to look at both the influence of identity on voting behaviour and the ways in which different social identities interact to either cross-cut or reinforce each other. In this as in the chapters which follow we try to set the position in Scotland within the comparative framework of the rest of Great Britain. Thus, not only are we concerned with the way these factors influence voting behaviour in Scotland but we are also interested in whether these factors operate differently in Scotland from elsewhere in Great Britain. For example, is the effect of feeling a sense of working class identity the same in Scotland as in England and Wales, or is there a greater tendency for those in Scotland who feel working class to support Labour?

The key questions we examine are:

- Does the social structure of Scotland explain voting behaviour in Scotland?
- Does social structure affect voting in Scotland in the same ways in which it affects voting south of the border?
- To what extent do social identities take precedence over social location as explanations of voting behaviour?
- In what ways do identities in Scotland overlap to reinforce or cross-cut each other?

CHANGES SINCE 1992

The 1997 general election in the UK ushered in the first Labour government since 1979 in dramatic style. However, the results in terms of the share of votes won by the parties were somewhat less dramatic. In this section we describe the changes that have occurred in voting behaviour between 1992 and 1997 to look at the extent to which the parties were able to hold onto their support and the directions of vote switching by the electorate. In Scotland, this is of special interest: the electorate have more options to choose among, and in many respects the policy positions of three of those parties are similar, and so we might expect to find greater vote switching within the Scottish electorate than elsewhere in Britain. Table 3.1 shows the breakdown of party support in 1992 by how each party's voters cast their votes in 1997[1].

---

[1] Here we must rely on the voter's recall of their vote at the 1992 election. This will contain some mis-reporting, with respondents more likely to claim that they voted and also more likely to recall voting for the same party in 1992 as in 1997. Therefore these results may overestimate stability in vote between the two elections.

As with all comparisons between Scotland and the rest of Britain, interpretation of the patterns are complicated by the presence of the SNP. When differences arise it is not always clear whether these are 'real' differences between Scotland and the rest of Britain, in terms of the impact of factors on voting behaviour, or whether any differences that are found are reflections of Scotland's different party system. Thus, we must be careful in our interpretations of relationships for other parties as we are not comparing like with like. However, bearing that in mind we can still make some useful comparisons between Scotland and the rest of Great Britain. One of the most striking features of Table 3.1 is the constant levels of non-voting in 1997 among supporters of different parties in 1992. An explanation that is sometimes offered for the fate of the Conservatives in Scotland in 1997 was that Conservative voters in 1992 were more likely to stay away from the polls in 1997. However, Table 3.1 shows quite clearly that this was not the case in Scotland or elsewhere in Britain, with around ten per cent of each party's 1992 support abstaining in 1997.

Table 3.1: **Vote in 1992 election by vote in 1997**

| | *1992 vote* | | | | | | | | |
| | Scotland | | | | | rest of Britain | | | |
	Did not Vote	Con	Lab	Lib Dem	SNP	Did not Vote	Con	Lab	Lib Dem
1997 vote									
Did not vote	52	10	10	9	10	58	10	11	13
Con	5	51	1	4	0	10	60	2	4
Lab	26	18	80	16	13	21	15	80	27
Lib Dem	3	13	3	69	4	10	11	6	51
SNP	10	6	6	0	73	-	-	-	-
Other	3	1	0	2	0	1	4	2	5
N (=100%)	117	156	315	63	105	360	908	818	262

Source: British Election Survey 1997.

Perhaps less surprisingly, in each of the groups of voters, Labour was the largest beneficiary of vote switching. There is also evidence of significant proportions of Conservative voters in 1992 moving directly to Labour voting in 1997. Previous work on vote switching had shown that where voters leave their usual party they do not do straight moves to the other major party but rather turn to a half-way house, like the Liberal Democrats. The fact that 18 per cent of Conservative voters in Scotland and 15 per cent in the rest of Britain switched directly from Conservative to Labour may be an indication of the success of 'New Labour' in attracting different kinds of voters.

There is little evidence to suggest that voters in Scotland were more volatile than those elsewhere in Britain, with 67 per cent of those in Scotland and 65 per cent of those in the rest of Britain behaving in the same manner at both elections (that is either voting for the same party at both elections or abstaining at both elections). Thus, despite the dramatic outcome of the election in producing a change of government, a majority of the electorate did not change their voting behaviour.

THE PATTERN OF PARTY SUPPORT

Stability of the vote between elections is one measure of the attachment of the electorate to parties; another measure is party identification. This measure was first developed in the American context (Campbell et al, 1960), and later imported to the British context in the first British Election Studies (Butler and Stokes, 1974). It is designed to measure the voters' long-term attachment to a party. As Butler and Stokes put it

> The values which the individual sees in supporting a party usually extend to more than one general election. ... As a result, most electors think of themselves as supporters of a given party in a lasting sense, developing what may be called a 'partisan self-image'.

It has been shown that this party identity, whilst a strong predictor of voting behaviour, does not move hand in hand with vote. Both in the American and British contexts, voters often cast their votes for a different party from the one they feel an attachment to. This may be for a variety of different reasons. In the American context, there may be strong candidate effects, such that an individual candidate appeals to people regardless of their party attachments. In the British context, there may be tactical reasons for the vote (which we will discuss below); there has also been some evidence of short-term movement from a party as a form of protest which usually results in people returning to their party of long-term attachment at subsequent elections. The fact that party identity and vote are not perfectly correlated suggests that the concept does tap into some long-term sense of attachment to parties, which endures even if the voter switches party for a specific election.

Table 3.2 looks at the voting behaviour of each group of party identifiers, including those who claimed to have no partisan identification. As the table shows, a majority of those who claim an identification with a party also voted for that party. What is of interest in this table is the mismatch between party identity and vote. This gives us some indication of the way in which people view other parties. Thus, in Scotland, SNP identifiers voted only for the SNP or the Labour Party, suggesting that there are commonalities among these parties that are not there for other partisan groups. Another feature of the table is the small proportions of identifiers with other parties who voted for the Conservatives. Fewer than five per cent of supporters of other parties claimed to have voted Conservative in 1997, an indication of the isolation of the Conservatives in 1997. The table shows that differences between Scotland and the rest of Britain are small.

A further way of assessing the extent to which parties are grouped together in the minds of the electorate is to look at the pattern of second choices among each group of voters. Table 3.3 looks at this relationship.

This table again shows quite clearly the relative isolation of the Conservative Party at the 1997 election. In both Scotland and the rest of Britain, less than one-fifth of the electorate chose the Conservative Party as their second preference. In Scotland we can again see the relative closeness of Labour and the SNP, with over 60 per cent of

Table   3.2:   Party   identity   and   vote

	party identity								
	Scotland					rest of Britain			
	None	Con	Lab	Lib Dem	SNP	None	Con	Lab	Lib Dem
1997 vote									
Did not vote	48	14	15	7	19	52	13	19	15
Con	6	63	0	4	0	6	74	0	3
Lab	14	7	80	8	12	22	4	75	12
Lib Dem	10	6	1	76	0	13	6	5	67
SNP	12	7	4	3	68	-	-	-	-
Other	10	2	0	1	0	7	3	1	4
N (=100%)	51	143	402	92	137	168	801	1130	325

Source: British Election Survey 1997.

Table   3.3:   Second   choice   party

	1997 vote						
	Scotland				rest of Britain		
	Con	Lab	Lib Dem	SNP	Con	Lab	Lib Dem
Second choice							
Con	-	6	17	8	-	12	24
Lab	24	-	54	68	28	-	70
Lib Dem	56	29	-	23	60	77	-
SNP	16	62	28	-	-	-	-
Other	4	3	1	2	12	10	6
N (=100%)	82	311	78	117	554	884	332

Source: British Election Survey 1997.

each party's voters giving the other as their second choice. Unsurprisingly, the majority of Conservative voters gave the Liberal Democrats as their second choice, although in Scotland 16 per cent said that their second choice would be the SNP.

A possible consequence of this isolation of the Conservative Party, and the conscious campaigning by the others parties on the workings of the electoral system, is a significant amount of 'tactical' voting. The result of the 1997 election in Scotland was particularly dramatic in the way the electoral system translated votes into seats. It is widely thought that an explanation for this was that many voters had voted tactically to ensure that Conservative seats were lost to whoever was the closest opposition (Curtice and Steed, 1997). We can test this proposition by looking at the reasons people gave for voting as they did; these are shown in Table 3.4. It shows that, for each party, the proportions claiming to have voted for reasons other than that they always vote that way or that they thought it was the best party are quite small. However, as we saw in Table 3.2, most of the electorate voted the same way in 1997 as in 1992 and so we should expect to find these reasons as predominant. Among the 'other' category, a large proportion gave reasons that could be read as 'tactical': for example, 'time for a change' or 'to defeat the Conservatives'. Thus if we take all the 'other' responses along with those who said they preferred another party, we see tactical voting at around 15 per cent of the electorate. Further analysis showed that of those who switched their vote between 1997 and 1992, around 30 per cent said they did so for tactical reasons (defined in these ways).

Again when looking at the reasons given for voting in Scotland as compared with the rest of Great Britain, we find that the differences are relatively small. In the rest of Britain the Liberal Democrats seem to have benefited from tactical voting, whilst in Scotland this is shared relatively evenly among Labour, the Liberal Democrats and the SNP. There is also evidence that the Conservatives have been driven back onto their core vote in Scotland to a greater extent than in the rest of Britain: 53 per cent of Scottish Conservative voters said they always voted Conservative, compared to 36 per cent in the rest of Britain.

Thus, in terms of change since 1992 and patterns of party support at the 1997 election, the differences between Scotland and the rest of

Britain are small. The Scots were no more likely to be vote switchers, despite having a greater number of choices available. In both Scotland and the rest of Britain, the Conservatives were relatively isolated, gaining very few second preferences. In neither Scotland nor the rest of Britain was there evidence to suggest that Conservative supporters were more likely than other party supporters to abstain from voting.

Table   3.4:   Reasons   for   vote

	1997 vote						
	Scotland				rest of Britain		
	Con	Lab	Lib Dem	SNP	Con	Lab	Lib Dem
reason for vote							
Always vote that way	53	29	14	39	36	28	8
Best party	43	55	67	38	50	61	57
Really preferred another party	1	12	9	9	7	7	20
Other	3	4	10	13	7	4	15
N (=100%)	99	352	87	128	622	984	358

Source: British Election Survey 1997.

SOCIAL STRUCTURE

We next look at the impact of social structure on voting behaviour. In a now infamous quote, Pulzer claimed that 'class is the basis of British party politics; all else is embellishment and detail' (Pulzer, 1967). During the 1950s and 1960s this was seen as an accurate portrayal of British politics. The last two decades have seen dramatic changes in the party system and have been referred to as an era of 'dealignment' in which voters have been freed from the constraint of class that had previously anchored them to parties (Sarlvik and Crewe, 1983). However, as we have already seen, even these supposedly 'free-floating' voters behave in a stable way across elections. In this section we outline the effects which social location, as measured by occupational class, housing tenure and educational level, still has on voting behaviour. We are also concerned to see if these effects vary in Scotland from the rest of Britain.

Tables 3.5, 3.6 and 3.7 show how each of these structural variables are related to voting behaviour. Table 3.5 shows that, although there remains some relationship between vote and social class[2], this is relatively weak. Here there appears to be some difference between Scotland and the rest of Britain: among all classes, Scotland has a lower proportion voting Conservative and, in all but the salariat, a higher proportion voting Labour. This is especially marked when we consider that the Labour Party in Scotland is competing in a four party system and so, if all else were equal, might be expected to get a lower share of the Scottish vote than in the rest of Britain.

It is clearly no longer the case, if it ever was, that voting behaviour can be explained solely in terms of class location. Amongst the salariat in England and Wales equal proportions voted for Labour and the Conservatives, whilst in Scotland a higher proportion of the salariat voted Labour than Conservative. SNP support among the different classes is not strongly differentiated. Although their support is lowest among the petty bourgeoisie and highest among the working class, the differences are small. This is despite conscious attempts by the SNP to promote its left-of-centre policy programme to try to capture the working class vote.

Table 3.6 repeats this analysis but for housing tenure. It has been argued that the spread of home ownership has led tenure to be of greater importance than social class in predicting voting behaviour, as home owners have a particular set of political priorities which distinguish them from the rest of the population (Rose and McAllister, 1986; Saunders, 1990). In the 1950s and 1960s, tenure was largely a reflection of social class, with the middle class owning property and the working class renting it. However, the spread of home ownership and the sale of council houses have led to a

---

[2] Here, and throughout, we are using the Goldthorpe-Heath social class groupings. See Heath et al (1985) for a discussion of the derivation of these groupings and their relevance to political behaviour.

Table 3.5: Social class and vote

social class

	Scotland					rest of Britain				
1997 vote	Salariat	Routine non-manual	Petty Bourgeoisie	Manual Foremen and Technicians	Working class	Salariat	Routine non-manual	Petty Bourgeoisie	Manual Foremen and Technicians	Working class
Did not vote	14	14	28	17	18	13	19	22	19	24
Con	22	9	18	7	2	33	27	34	15	14
Lab	28	47	30	51	54	33	37	28	48	49
Lib Dem	19	12	12	7	7	18	14	13	14	11
SNP	14	17	12	17	18	-	-	-	-	-
Other	2	1	0	0	1	3	3	3	4	3
N (=100%)	203	177	48	70	284	755	512	223	160	767

Source: British Election Survey 1997.

Table 3.6: Housing tenure and vote

	housing tenure							
	Scotland				rest of Britain			
1997 vote	Owns	Rent: Local Authority	Rent: Housing Association	Rent: Other	Owns	Rent: Local Authority	Rent: Housing Association	Rent: Other
Did not vote	16	19	18	19	16	28	26	34
Conservative	15	3	4	19	29	7	13	20
Labour	39	52	54	40	37	55	42	30
Liberal Democrat	14	6	0	11	15	6	14	16
SNP	14	20	21	8	-	-	-	-
Other	1	0	4	2	3	3	5	1
N (=100%)	485	259	40	36	1789	410	96	195

Source: British Election Survey 1997.

Table 3.7: Educational qualifications and vote

educational qualifications

	Scotland						rest of Britain					
	Degree	Higher education below degree	A level or equiv.*	O level or equiv.**	CSE or equiv.	No qualifications	Degree	Higher education below degree	A level or equiv.*	O level or equiv.**	CSE or equiv.	No qualifications
1997 vote												
Did not vote	11	14	18	20	21	16	14	16	23	18	24	20
Con	22	15	8	14	5	9	23	32	27	30	17	20
Lab	25	32	49	41	53	50	38	28	34	34	46	46
Lib Dem	29	20	12	7	9	5	22	21	15	14	10	10
SNP	10	15	13	18	12	18	-	-	-	-	-	-
Other	2	4	0	0	0	1	3	3	2	3	2	3
N (=100%)	75	111	145	152	61	281	267	337	269	433	298	892

* includes Scottish Higher grade.

** includes Scottish O grade and Standard Grade, and GCSE.

Source: British Election Survey 1997.

weakening of the relationship between class and tenure, allowing tenure to have an independent impact on voting behaviour.

Table 3.6 shows much the same pattern as for social class. However, the differentials between different tenure groups seem to be larger than for social class groups. In Scotland, Labour and the SNP do particularly well amongst those living in accommodation rented from local authorities and housing associations. In contrast the Conservatives do not do as well among owner occupiers as we might have expected, gaining just 15 per cent of the votes of this group in Scotland, and 29 per cent in the rest of Britain. Because of the small number of cases in the sample, it is not possible to investigate the reasons for this, but a possibility could be the proportions within the owner occupiers who had purchased their homes from a local authority. In Scotland, 28 per cent of owner occupiers had bought their home from a local authority compared with 13 per cent in the rest of Britain.

The final measure of social location which we look at is educational qualifications. This has been termed a 'post-industrial' influence on voting behaviour, as it focuses on the knowledge dimension of society and is related to the growth of the service sector in the economy (Harrop and Miller, 1987). In general terms, what has been found is that the better educated members of a society are more politically active, are more liberal in their attitudes and have greater tolerance of new ideas and minority groups. We might expect these characteristics to manifest themselves in voting behaviour through higher turnout and a greater tendency to vote for the more liberal parties. Table 3.7 looks at the relationship between voting behaviour and education level.

Table 3.7 shows some evidence of these influences. Those with degree level qualification or higher education below degree level are more likely to vote for the Liberal Democrats, apparently largely at the expense of the Labour Party among these groups. There is also some relationship between level of education and likelihood to vote. However, this relationship, like that of housing tenure and social class, is relatively weak and would not provide a good method of predicting voting behaviour in Scotland or in the rest of Britain.

We must conclude, therefore, that while social location does still have an impact on voting behaviour it is by no means its sole determinant. In addition, although it is problematic to make direct comparisons between Scotland and the rest of Britain (because of the presence of the SNP), there do not appear to be any substantial differences in the impact of these variables on voting behaviour.

Before turning to social identity, we consider two further measures of social location, age and gender. These are unlike the other measure of social location in that they are less obviously politicised and are not, themselves, affected by government policy. However, these variables have, in the past, been found to have an influence on voting behaviour. The young are usually considered to be less conservative (in both social and moral attitudes) and thus less likely to vote for the Conservative Party, and there has historically been a 'gender gap' in voting behaviour with women being more likely to vote Conservative. We look at these relationship at the 1997 general election in Tables 3.8 and 3.9.

Table 3.8 suggests that there is no clear relationship between age and voting behaviour: although there are some differences these do not operate in a linear manner. The key difference between age groups is not which party was chosen but whether people voted at all, with the under-35s especially unlikely to vote. In Scotland, the Conservative vote shows little tendency to increase with age, whilst the Labour vote is marginally higher amongst the younger age groups. However, the difference between Scotland and the rest of Britain is marked amongst the older age groups, where Conservative support is considerably higher in England and Wales.

Table 3.9 shows that there is no evidence for a gender gap, of any kind, differences between males and females being small in both Scotland and the rest of Britain.

To summarise: we have found only weak relationships between social location measures and voting behaviour. None of the measures included here provides a good predictor of voting behaviour. In addition, where differences between Scotland and the rest of Britain can be discerned, these are generally small. This suggests that these influences operate in similar ways in Scotland and in England and Wales.

Table 3.8: **Age and vote**

	age						
	18-24	25-34	35-44	45-54	55-59	60-64	65+
1997 vote (Scotland)							
Did not vote	23	22	21	11	16	11	14
Con	10	3	8	17	5	16	20
Lab	44	53	39	38	47	41	42
Lib Dem	11	5	16	11	14	12	12
SNP	12	17	14	21	19	16	11
Other	1	1	1	1	0	4	1
N (=100%)	76	159	146	420	157	62	189
1997 vote (rest of Britain)							
Did not vote	33	27	20	14	11	12	12
Con	18	19	21	25	33	28	32
Lab	32	37	40	43	40	44	38
Lib Dem	16	13	15	16	15	11	14
Other	0	3	4	2	1	4	4
N (=100%)	176	472	500	420	157	192	598

Source: British Election Survey 1997.

SOCIAL IDENTITY

Scotland, in recent years, has seen renewed interest in social identities as an explanation of voting behaviour. Ever since the first studies of voting behaviour in Britain, class identity has had a closer relationship

Table 3.9:   Gender and vote

	Scotland		rest of Britain	
	Male	Female	Male	Female
1997 vote				
Did not vote	18	16	21	18
Conservative	11	12	23	26
Labour	43	43	39	39
Liberal Democrat	9	14	14	14
SNP	17	14	-	-
Other	2	1	3	2
N (=100%)	356	482	1173	1350

Source: British Election Survey 1997.

to vote than the social class to which respondents were allocated by
social researchers (Butler and Stokes, 1974). Those who considered
themselves to be working class were more likely to support Labour
and those who thought of themselves as middle class more likely to
vote Conservative. This is hardly surprising: we would expect to find
that a person's own sense of their social location would have greater
predictive power than an externally imposed measure. In Scotland,
levels of working class identity have tended to be higher than
elsewhere in Britain (Brand et al, 1995) even after the occupational
breakdown is taken into account. Thus one possible explanation for
the higher Labour vote in Scotland could be this greater sense of
working class identity.

    In addition to class identity, religion has traditionally been an
important influence on voting behaviour in Scotland. The
Conservative Party could mobilise a large working-class Protestant
vote, whilst Catholics in Scotland were overwhelmingly Labour
voters. If, as has been suggested (Seawright and Curtice, 1995), this
link between the Conservatives and the working-class Protestant vote

has been declining, we may have an explanation for the poor performance of the Conservatives in Scotland in recent elections.

Since the early 1970s and the rise of popular support for the SNP, national identity has grown alongside religious and class identities as an explanation for the Scottish vote. As we will see in Chapter Four, the strength of national identity, and the way in which the parties are perceived as being Scottish or otherwise, are crucial elements in understanding party fortunes in Scotland. Popular accounts of both the general election, and the subsequent referendum, placed a considerable emphasis on national identity as the key variable in understanding the demise of the Conservatives at the general election and the clear Yes votes in the referendum. However, as we will see in Chapter Six, the explanation for the referendum result does not lie with national sentiment. In this section we assess if the result of the general election is explicable in terms of identity.

Before we turn to the effect these identities have on voting behaviour in Scotland, we look at the ways in which these identities cross-cut or reinforce each other. Sociologists have long recognised that an individual's identity is often made up of a complex array of competing and often contradictory identities (Hall, 1992). Thus we begin by assessing how these multiple identities in Scotland interact with each other. Tables 3.10 and 3.11 look at how class and religious identities are related to national identity[3]; data for England[4] are provided for comparison purposes.

Table 3.10 shows that in England almost half of the electorate place themselves at the centre of this scale of national identity: that is,

---

[3] Here, we are using the questions 'Which religion do you feel you belong to', 'Do you belong to any social class' and a scale of responses on national identity as shown in Table 3.10. This national identity question is sometimes referred to as the 'Moreno question', after Luis Moreno who first used it (Moreno, 1988).

[4] In this table we exclude the small number of Welsh cases as national identity in Wales is rather different to that in England. We recognise that the meaning of this measure of national identity may be different in England. See Heath and Kellas (1998) for a discussion of these national identities.

they say that they are equally English and British. This is in sharp contrast with Scotland, where over 50 per cent state they are either 'Scottish and not British' or 'Scottish more than British'. In England, the measure of national identity varies very little with class identity. In Scotland, however, there is more variation with class identity. Those who consider themselves to be working class (an overwhelming majority of the Scots electorate at 71 per cent) are more likely to adopt a predominately Scottish national identity: that is, they are more likely to say that they are 'Scottish and not British' or 'Scottish more than British'. Those who say that they are middle class are more likely to hold a British identity (though these remain very much a minority even among the middle class).

Table   3.10:   National   identity   and   class   identity

	class identity			
	Scotland		England	
	Middle class	Working class	Middle class	Working class
national identity				
Scottish/English not British	17	26	7	8
Scottish/English more than British	33	42	20	17
Scottish/English equal to British	34	26	45	52
British more than Scottish/English	10	2	19	13
British not Scottish/English	6	3	10	9
N (=100%)	205	590	852	1358

Source: British Election Survey 1997.

Table 3.11 shows differences in national identity among the religious groups are smaller, but nevertheless greater than in England. Those who say they do not belong to a religion are most likely to hold a predominately Scottish national identity, though the differences

Table 3.11: National identity and religion

religion

national identity	Scotland				England			
	No religion	Catholic	Protestant	Other	No religion	Catholic	Protestant	Other
Scottish/English not British	30	24	20	21	8	8	8	4
Scottish/English more than British	37	39	41	40	19	14	20	12
Scottish/English equal to British	23	27	32	29	49	46	51	45
British more than Scottish/English	4	5	4	10	14	16	15	16
British not Scottish/English	5	5	3	2	9	16	6	23
N (=100%)	244	118	391	56	711	222	1153	188

Source: British Election Survey 1997.

are not great. Perhaps surprisingly – given the historical association between Protestantism and British Unionism – the differences between Catholics and Protestants are small.

The tables suggest that identities in Scotland are both crosscutting and reinforcing. Social class identity and national identity seem to reinforce each other, whilst national identity and religion appear to be to some extent cross-cutting – that is to say relatively independent of each other.

What impact do these identities have on voting behaviour in Scotland? Tables 3.12, 3.13 and 3.14 show how each of these identities is related to vote. Again we provide data for the rest of Britain for comparison purposes. For class identity (Table 3.12), there is a very clear – though by no means deterministic – relationship between class identity and voting behaviour. The Conservatives do considerably better amongst those who think of themselves as middle class, in both Scotland and elsewhere, though overall levels of support are lower in Scotland. Labour do very well amongst those who consider themselves to be working class, gaining almost half of the votes of this group. It is worth pointing out here that the proportion of the electorate who say that they are working class is lower in the rest of Britain (60 per cent compared with 71 per cent in Scotland). Thus, one possible explanation for the strength of Labour in Scotland could be a greater prevalence of 'working class' communities, the traditional source of support for Labour.

When we consider the relationship between vote and religion (Table 3.13), we can see that the historical link between Labour and Catholic voters in Scotland remains, with Labour gaining two-thirds of the Catholic vote. However, the Conservatives do not do so well among Protestant voters: although this is the religious group with the highest Conservative vote, it remains at only 17 per cent.

For national identity and vote (Table 3.14), we find that in England there is almost no relationship between voting behaviour and national identity; this may be explained by the fact that national identity is not politicised south of the border. In Scotland, however, we find a very clear relationship. As we might expect, the Conservatives poll very badly among those with a predominately Scottish identity, gaining just five per cent of the vote among those who feel 'Scottish and not

Table   3.12:   Class   identity   and   vote

	class identity			
	Scotland		rest of Britain	
	Middle class	Working class	Middle class	Working class
1997 vote				
Did not vote	10	20	15	21
Conservative	24	6	38	16
Labour	31	49	27	47
Liberal Democrat	20	8	17	13
SNP	13	16	-	-
Other	3	0	3	3
N (=100%)	212	596	940	1508

Source: British Election Survey 1997.

British' and eight per cent among those who feel 'Scottish more than British'; as we have already seen, these groups comprise about half of the Scottish electorate. Again as we might have expected, the SNP poll highest among those with an exclusive Scottish identity. Labour do well amongst all groups, but their support is lower among the minority of the Scottish electorate who felt more British than Scottish.

Tables 3.12, 3.13 and 3.14 suggest that the relationship between identity and voting behaviour is stronger than that between social location and voting behaviour. We also find more evidence here for differences between Scotland and the rest of Britain – though this is perhaps due to the way in which identities have been politicised in Scotland and not so obviously mobilised in England.

MODELS OF VOTING

In the final section of this chapter, we try to assess the relative importance of these different factors in explaining voting behaviour. Thus, we use multi-variate analysis to assess the impact of all of these

Table 3.13: **Religion and vote**

religion

1997 vote	Scotland				rest of Britain			
	No religion	Catholic	Protestant	Other	No religion	Catholic	Protestant	Other
Did not vote	22	17	14	19	27	16	15	19
Conservative	7	4	17	11	16	18	33	20
Labour	42	66	38	36	38	49	37	46
Liberal Democrat	10	3	13	22	16	15	13	13
SNP	18	8	17	10	-	-	-	-
Other	1	1	1	3	3	3	3	2
N (=100%)	249	121	403	65	807	251	1238	227

Source: British Election Survey 1997.

Table 3.14: National identity and vote

	national identity									
	Scotland					England				
1997 vote	Scottish not British	Scottish more than British	Scottish and British equally	British more than Scottish	British not Scottish	English not British	English more than British	English and British equally	British more than English	British not English
Did not vote	18	17	17	14	17	20	19	20	15	16
Conservative	5	8	19	19	21	25	28	26	29	18
Labour	48	44	41	35	38	38	34	38	36	43
Liberal Democrat	7	13	11	16	14	16	16	13	16	17
SNP	22	18	10	8	7	-	-	-	-	-
Other	-	1	2	8	3	1	3	2	4	6
N (=100%)	191	323	223	35	30	185	390	1099	347	209

Source: British Election Survey 1997.

measures simultaneously. Table 3.15 shows the result of multi-variate logistic regression analyses of voting behaviour. (Details of this technique are in the Appendix. The sample numbers are too small to allow reliable modelling of Liberal Democrat voting.) For ease of presentation, we indicate which variables are significant and their direction of influence on vote.

These models of party support confirm the findings above; in particular, many of the variables are not significant predictors of party support. We also begin to see some difference between Scotland and the rest of Britain which are not obvious from the tabular analysis. As the tables showed, the three measures of social location – social class, housing tenure and education – are only relatively weak influences on voting behaviour in Scotland, though they (especially education) have a slightly stronger influence in the rest of Britain. It is interesting to note that, in the rest of Britain, the Labour vote is only weakly related to social class and – unlike in Scotland – is not in any way a product of differential support amongst the working class. This may be an indication of the way in which 'New Labour' in England attempted to become a catch-all party not tied to a specific class group. In both Scotland and the rest of Britain, religion has an impact on Labour voting, with Catholics more likely to be Labour voters.

At first the influence of national identity appears curious. It appears to be stronger in the rest of Britain than in Scotland. This can be explained by the reference category used and by the small numbers of the sample in the 'British' categories in Scotland. Thus, in Scotland it is not a significant predictor of Labour support as Labour support is similar in the three groups 'Scottish not British', 'Scottish more than British' and 'Scottish equal to British'. The groups which have a lower tendency to support Labour have such small numbers of respondents that the coefficients, whilst large, are not statistically significant.

Support for the SNP is not related to measures of social location. However, it has some relationship with identity as Catholics are less likely to be SNP voters, as are those who do not prioritise their Scottish identity over their British identity.

Table 3.15: Models of vote

Variables (reference category in brackets)	Scotland			rest of Britain	
	Con	Lab	SNP	Con	Lab
Gender (Male)					
Female					
Social class (Salariat)					
Routine non-manual		+			
Petty Bourgoisie					-
Manual				-	
Foremen/Technicians					
Working class	--	++		--	
Insufficient info.					-
Housing Tenure (Owner)					
Rents: Local Authority	--			--	++
Rents: Housing Association	+				
Other					
Education qualifications (Degree)					
Higher education, non-degree				++	--
A level or equiv.				++	-
O level or equiv.				++	--
CSE or equiv.					
No qualifications				+	
Other				+	
Class identity (Non-working class)					
Working class identity	--	+		--	++
National identity (Scottish/English not British)					
Scottish/English more than British	+			++	--
Scottish/English equal to British			-	++	--
British more than Scottish/English				++	-
British not Scottish/English					

[Table 3.15 continued on next page]

[Table 3.15 continued]

	Scotland			rest of Britain	
	Con	Lab	SNP	Con	Lab
Religion (Protestant)					
Catholic		++	-		++
Other					++
Age (in years)	++			++	

+ *indicates significant positive effect (at 5% level)*
++ *indicates significant positive effect (at 1% level)*
- *indicates significant negative effect (at 5% level)*
-- *indicates significant negative effect (at 1% level)*
Source: British Election Survey 1997.

CONCLUSION

In this chapter we have used data from the 1997 British Election Survey to outline further the background to the 1997 election. We have seen that, despite the dramatic result, the majority of the electorate behaved in the same way as in 1992. We have also seen the relative isolation of the Conservatives, in both Scotland and the rest of Britain, and the likely impact this had on the result through the use of tactical voting.

In considering the influences on voting behaviour, we found relatively weak influences of social structure, and few differences in this respect between Scotland and the rest of Britain. Thus, in the next chapter and in Chapter Five we try to find other explanations for the distinctiveness of the election results in Scotland. If Scotland's social structure doesn't explain the weak position of the Conservatives in Scotland, what does?

A partial explanation can be found in the feelings of identity held by the Scottish electorate, where those who feel Scottish are much less likely to be Conservative supporters. However, this is not the whole story as Chapter Four will show.

4

Political Values

INTRODUCTION

In Chapter Three we looked at one aspect of the political debate in Scotland – the idea that voting patterns in Scotland are inextricably linked to a complex array of social identities. In this and the following chapter we turn our attention to political values and attitudes in order to investigate Scottish distinctiveness and the sources of any differences. A distinction is often drawn in the academic literature between political attitudes and political values (Feldman, 1988), with attitudes and opinions being the application of value systems to policy issues. Thus, in this chapter we focus on value systems in Scotland, whilst Chapter Five looks at policy preferences.

Throughout the existing literature on political behaviour in Scotland runs a single key theme – is Scotland different? (Dickson, 1989; Brown et al, 1996). Undoubtedly, in recent years political behaviour in Scotland (as measured by voting behaviour and popular opinion) has diverged from the 'British' norm. As shown in Chapter Two, general elections in Scotland have been dominated by the Labour Party at a time when the Conservatives enjoyed electoral dominance in England. Although the 1997 election appears to have realigned Scottish and English voting patterns, the presence of the SNP and the failure of the Conservatives to win a single Scottish seat mean that Scottish distinctiveness cannot be ignored. The electoral divergence between Scotland and the rest of Great Britain has led to a widespread belief that political values in Scotland must be different. The electoral dominance of left-of-centre parties and the failure of the Conservatives seem to suggest that people in Scotland hold more left-wing and collectivist values than people elsewhere in Britain.

In this chapter we evaluate these claims. We focus on three key issues:

- Are political values in Scotland different from those in the rest of Great Britain?
- Do political values explain voting behaviour in Scotland?
- Does Scotland have a distinct 'political culture'?

VALUE SYSTEMS

Value (or belief) systems are the underlying principles which structure political opinions. They are the principles which guide individuals to specific policy preferences and which aid individuals in making sense of political information. In his now classic article on belief systems amongst the American public, Converse (1964, p.207) defines a belief system as 'a configuration of ideas and attitudes in which the elements are bound together by some form of constraint'. He goes on to explain constraint as: 'the success we would have in predicting, given initial knowledge that an individual holds a specified attitude, that he holds certain further ideas and attitudes'.

In this way attitudes cluster together to form value systems. For example, we might expect an individual who believes in equalising incomes to believe also in greater taxation of the rich. Or we may expect an individual who believes in free speech to be also against regulation of films and magazines. In general, we would expect positions on these value systems to be stable over time, such that, whilst individuals' specific policy preferences might change, the underlying principles which structure these preferences will be stable. To be strictly correct, we should say we are looking, not at values directly in the sense that a moral philosopher would understand them, but at measurable expressions of values. However, in keeping with most of the political science literature on this topic, we do refer to these measurable expressions as values.

Early research on political attitudes in Britain tended to focus on the measurement of single attitudes as indicators of 'core' beliefs: for example attitudes towards nationalisation could be used to measure underlying positions on a left-right value system. Butler and Stokes (1974), in the first national election study in Britain, concluded that attitudes exhibited such low levels of stability over time as to call into question the very notion of core beliefs amongst the British public. They found that individuals would take different positions on the same issue at different times and that attitudes that would appear to form clusters at an ideological level were only weakly associated at the individual level.

However, more recent work has suggested that measurement of core beliefs using individual questionnaire items is dogged by problems of context and question wording. Using more sophisticated techniques of factor analysis, Heath et al (1994) demonstrate that scales can be constructed which do show stability over time and which therefore suggest that value systems do exist amongst the British public. The scales developed by Heath et al identify two dimensions to political opinion, the socialist-laissez faire (or left-right) dimension and a liberal-authoritarian dimension. These two scales were specifically designed and tested in a British context, and so we use them here to represent the underlying value systems in Britain and to investigate the supposed differences in beliefs in Scotland and the rest of Britain.

VALUE SCALES

The two scales are each constructed from six questionnaire items included in the election surveys. The items are:

Socialist-Laissez faire
- Ordinary people get their fair share of the nation's wealth.
- There is one law for the rich and one for the poor.
- There is no need for strong trade unions to protect employees' working conditions and pay.
- It is the government's responsibility to provide a job for everyone who wants one.
- Private enterprise is the best way to solve Britain's economic problems.
- Major public services and industries ought to be in state ownership.

Liberal-Authoritarian

- Young people today don't have enough respect for traditional British values.
- Censorship of films and magazines is necessary to uphold moral standards.
- People in Britain should be more tolerant of those who lead unconventional lifestyles.
- Homosexual relations are always wrong.
- People should be allowed to organise public meetings to protest against the government.
- Even political parties that wish to overthrow democracy should not be banned.

In each case the possible responses were Strongly Agree, Agree, Neither, Disagree, Strongly Disagree. The items have be recoded so that they are in the same direction (for example, so that liberal responses all correspond to the 'agree' end of the responses), and then added together to produce two scales with a range of six to 30. Low values on the scales represent the socialist and liberal positions respectively.

In addition to these two scales a third scale which measures British nationalism was constructed. This scale provides a useful summary measure of a political dimension that appears to be taking on increasing importance in British politics (Heath et al, forthcoming); it measures attitudes towards British state nationalism. The items used in constructing this scale were as follows; we use Heath et al's label 'nationalist-cosmopolitan', although – as we will see – dissenting from the British nationalist positions might entail supporting a different form of nationalism (such as Scottish nationalism) rather than a rejection of any nationalism at all.

Nationalist-Cosmopolitan

- Britain has a lot to learn from other countries in running its affairs.
- I would rather be a citizen of Britain than any other country in the world.

- There are some things about Britain today that make me ashamed to be British.
- People in Britain are too ready to criticise their country.
- The government of Britain should do everything it can to keep all parts of Britain together in a single state.
- Britain should co-operate with other countries, even if it means giving up some independence.

Again, the six items had response categories ranging from strongly agree to strongly disagree and were aggregated to form a scale running from six through to 30 with six indicating a strong British nationalist position.

IS SCOTLAND DIFFERENT?

The scales described above measure three dimensions of 'core' beliefs among the British public. These scales provide more stringent measures of Scottish difference than responses to individual items. However, as discussed in Chapter Five, we recognise that positions taken on individual policy items are of great importance in understanding the differences between Scotland and the rest of Great Britain. Our contention here is that these underlying dimensions of political beliefs are of equal importance as they not only structure policy preferences but also give an indication of the 'political culture' of a society.

In this sense 'political culture' or 'ethos' is the 'set of widely shared beliefs, values and norms concerning the relationship of citizens to their government and to one and other' (McClosky and Zaller, 1984, p.17). As McClosky and Zaller go on to point out, the political culture itself may have real consequences for a nation:

> It clearly matters greatly to the political life of a nation whether its prevailing ideas favour democracy or authoritarianism, laissez-faire or socialism. ... Cultural traditions, once formed, take on a life of their own and can influence events in countless ways.

The political culture structures and is structured by the attitudes and opinions of citizens, through the rhetoric and political discourse of the society.

In this chapter we use the three scales described above as a means of measuring the 'political culture' of Scotland and the rest of Great Britain in order to assess the extent to which Scotland does have a distinct political culture. There are many reasons why we might expect Scotland to be distinct in this respect. The political culture in Scotland may be different to that in the rest of Britain because of a different political discourse and rhetoric, which is in turn supported by the institutions of civil society and in particular the Scottish media. The presence of a fourth political party with both a strong nationalist and a socialist agenda may also have an impact on the political culture. We begin, then, by looking for evidence of a distinctive political culture in Scotland.

Table 4.1 shows the average values of each of the scales in Scotland as compared with the rest of Great Britain as a whole and its component regions. This is an important comparison as it has been suggested by other work that while Scotland is distinct from the rest of Great Britain as a whole it is similar to some of the regions of England or to Wales (Curtice, 1988). The table also looks at the extent to which Scotland itself can be viewed as a homogeneous political culture by looking at regional differences within Scotland. As Table 4.1 indicates, Scotland is different from the rest of Great Britain on all three of the scales, being more socialist, more liberal and less British nationalist. When we turn to look at the regions of England, again Scotland is distinct, with the differences being greatest on the socialist-laissez faire scale and the nationalism scale. No region of England is more socialist than Scotland and all but the North West, Yorkshire and Humberside and East Anglia are significantly more laissez-faire (right wing). On the scale of nationalist sentiment (towards the British state) no region is less nationalistic than Scotland – with only the North West, East Anglia and London not being significantly more nationalistic than Scotland. There are fewer differences on the liberal-authoritarian scale, with only the West Midlands being significantly different from Scotland. There are no differences between Scotland and Wales. These results suggest that

Table 4.1: Average positions on value scales

	Socialist-Laissez faire	Liberal-Authoritarian	Nationalist-Cosmopolitan	N
Scotland	14.51	18.55	16.73	852
Rest of Great Britain	15.52*	18.99*	15.74*	2570
North	15.62*	19.02	15.27*	186
North West	14.58	18.76	16.47	247
Yorkshire and Humberside	14.99	19.25	15.68*	248
West Midlands	15.58*	19.61*	15.07*	284
East Midlands	15.75*	19.00	15.75*	211
East Anglia	15.47	18.35	16.65	148
South West	15.74*	19.23	15.48*	237
South East	16.13*	19.12	15.54*	546
Greater London	15.83*	18.26	16.31	290
Wales	14.28	18.96	15.83	173
Scottish Regions				
West Central	13.59*	18.50	16.78	357
East Central	15.02	18.26	16.79	254
North East	15.64	18.58	16.64	118
Outlying	14.58	19.27	16.73	123

Source: British Election Survey 1997.

Low values on the scales mean (respectively): more left-wing, more liberal, and more British nationalist.

* indicates a statistically significant (at 5%) difference between Scotland and the marked region on this scale.

The Scottish regions are defined in terms of local council areas as: **West Central** *is East Ayrshire, East Dunbartonshire, East Renfrewshire, Glasgow, Inverclyde, North Ayrshire, North Lanarkshire, Renfrewshire, South Ayrshire, South Lanarkshire, West Dunbartonshire;* **East Central** *is Clackmannanshire, East Lothian, Edinburgh, Falkirk, Fife, Midlothian, Stirling, West Lothian;* **North East** *is Aberdeen, Aberdeenshire, Angus, Dundee, Moray, Perth and Kinross;* **Outlying** *is Argyll and Bute, Comhairle nan Eilean, Dumfries and Galloway, Highland, Orkney, Borders, Shetland.*

there are significant differences between Scotland and England, which are not explicable by regional variation within England. Moreover, they suggest that differences occur on the values where we might expect Scotland to be different – socialism and British nationalism. We return to why these differences occur below.

Looking at Scotland itself, the figures seem to suggest that there is in fact relatively little regional variation in these value scales. With the exception of the socialist scale (on which the West Central region of Scotland is significantly more socialist), there are no significant regional differences in values. This suggests that there may be a homogeneous political culture throughout Scotland – although we must be cautious about drawing conclusions as these are based on relatively small samples in the individual Scottish regions.

Given the evidence in Table 4.1, we are left with the question: if Scotland is indeed different, then why is it different? In other words what factors influence people's position on the value scales and why is Scotland's position different?

WHERE DO VALUES COME FROM?

Converse (1964) identifies a number of sources of 'constraint' on people's beliefs – that is a number of ways in which values hold together. He identifies logical constraints, psychological constraints and social constraints. We are not concerned here with logical or psychological constraint as these cannot be used to explain differences in value systems within Great Britain; thus we are concerned with social sources of constraint. Within this category, Converse identifies two key ways in which social constraints operate. First, there are constraints arising from membership of social groups, or, to put it another way, constraints arising from social structure. Second, there are constraints arising from the way in which value systems are packaged together by elites. So, for example, there is no necessary link between left-wing views and Scottish nationalism but these have been linked together by both the SNP and the Labour Party in political discourse in Scotland.

We turn first to issues of social structure. One possible explanation of the differences in values between Scotland and the rest of Great Britain is that Scotland has a different social structure. So, it might be argued, Scotland has fewer middle class professionals and so is necessarily going to be less right-wing in its beliefs than elsewhere.

Table 4.2 investigates this idea – to test if the differences in values seen in Table 4.1 are explicable in terms of the social structure of Scotland. Table 4.2 presents the results of a series of regression models of positions on the three scales. Model I begins by assessing if Scotland is different by estimating a model which controls only for whether or not the respondent was resident in Scotland. Model II takes into account the effect of social structures in an objective sense (social class, housing tenure, gender, age and educational level); this model checks to see if the differences in values can be explained by differences in the types of people living in Scotland. Model III adds in the effect of class identity and religion. Earlier research (Brand et al, 1994) has shown that people in Scotland are more likely than their English counterparts to adopt a working class identity (see Chapter Three); this model assesses whether or not it is this more working class culture which leads to a more left-wing value system in Scotland. Finally, Model IV tests for the effect of national identity on values. This uses a question in the survey which asked respondents to say whether they felt themselves to belong to any of a list of national groupings. The options offered were (in this order) 'British, English, European, Irish, Northern Irish, Scottish, Welsh, Other, None of these'. People found no difficulty answering this, and in naming more than one identity. Thus, 79 per cent said they were Scottish, 52 per cent British, nine per cent European, and four per cent English; the other categories attracted negligible proportions. Among the Scottish identifiers, 45 per cent said they were also British and seven per cent European. Among the British, 14 per cent said they were also European.

As we are interested in Scottish differences, the table displays the coefficient from the models that measures the impact of being resident in Scotland. In each case this is the effect of living in Scotland after the other variables have been taken into consideration.

The coefficients from Model I confirm the findings in Table 4.1: Scotland is markedly more left-wing than the rest of Great Britain, somewhat more liberal and markedly less nationalistic in its attitudes towards the British state. By comparing the coefficients of Model II

Table 4.2:   **Scotland difference in models of value systems**

		model		
	I	II	III	IV
dependent variable				
Socialist-	-1.00	-0.68	-0.57	-0.01
Laissez faire	(0.16)	(0.16)	(0.16)	(0.28)
Liberal-	-0.44	-0.18	-0.17	-0.01
Authoritarian	(0.15)	(0.14)	(0.14)	(0.25)
Nationalist-	0.99	0.92	0.88	0.69
Cosmopolitan	(0.14)	(0.14)	(0.14)	(0.23)

Source: British Election Survey 1997.

The table shows the regression coefficient in an ordinary linear regression (and its standard error) for the dichotomous variable representing Scotland.

Negative values on the first two scales mean that Scotland is (respectively) more left wing and more liberal; positive values on the third scale mean that Scotland is less British nationalist.

Key to models:

I   *Scotland variable only.*

II   *Add social structure (sex, age, social class, housing tenure, education level).*

III   *Add class identity and religion.*

IV   *Add national identity.*

with those of Model I we can see if these differences are explicable by social structure. The impact of the social structural variables is very different on the three scales. The coefficient for the socialist-laissez faire (or left-right) scale is substantially reduced by introducing the structural variables, although it remains statistically significant. That is to say that, even after controlling for social structure, those living in Scotland are more left-wing in their values than those in the rest of Great Britain: for instance, a middle class person in Scotland tends to be more left-wing than a middle-class person in the rest of Britain. The coefficient for the liberal-authoritarian scale is reduced such that it is no longer statistically significant; this suggests that the difference found in Table 4.1, in which Scotland is more liberal than the rest of Great Britain, is explicable in terms of differences in social structure, and that Scotland appears more liberal simply because it has more of those social groups which tend to be liberal. Finally the coefficient for the nationalist scale is barely affected by the introduction of structural variables to the model. This suggests that attitudes on this dimension are largely unrelated to social structure.

The introduction of working class identity, in Model III, further reduces the coefficient for the socialist-laissez faire scale, although again this remains highly significant. The coefficients on the other two scales are not markedly affected. The final model, Model IV, takes into account national identity. Here we find a very large reduction in the coefficient for Scotland on the socialist-laissez faire scale, such that it is no longer statistically significant: that is (for example), a major reason why middle-class people in Scotland are more left-wing is that they identify themselves as Scottish rather than British (or English). The coefficient for the liberal-authoritarian scale remains non-significant. The coefficient for the nationalist scale is reduced but remains significant; this means that even people in Scotland who regard themselves as British are less likely to be British nationalist than people in the rest of Britain.

These models suggest that the value systems outlined above are representing different dimension of the political culture, because they are affected in different ways by the introduction of social group variables. It would seem that Scotland's apparent left-wing position can be explained in part by social structure but also by a sense of national identity. The more liberal position of Scotland can be explained by the social structure but the less nationalistic position towards the British state cannot wholly be explained by either the social structure or by a sense of national identity.

These findings bring us back to Converse's idea of constraint and the sources of constraint. In terms of the liberal-authoritarian scale, social sources of constraint appear to explain differences between Scotland and the rest of Great Britain. Once we take into account the different types of people living in the two areas these differences disappear. However, in the case of the other two scales social structure forms only a small part of the story and so we must look for other sources of constraint to explain these differences. Here we can turn to the second of Converse's social sources of constraint – the elite discourse and the way in which ideas are presented to the general public.

Political discourse in Great Britain is dominated by political parties. In Scotland, this has had a distinctive flavour because of the presence of the SNP. Since 1970, the SNP has consistently won at least ten per cent of the popular vote in Scotland and has had a prominent position in political coverage in Scotland. Since 1974, the party has adopted an explicitly left-wing standpoint in an attempt to compete more directly with the Labour Party in Scotland. The success with which this has been achieved can be seen in Table 4.3 which shows the perception of voters of the position of the SNP since 1974. The table clearly shows that the perception of the SNP changed. Unfortunately the question wording in the 1974 questionnaire does not allow a distinction to be made between those who thought the SNP were equally placed between Labour and the Conservatives and those who felt unable to give a placement. However, the evidence does suggest that since 1979 the SNP are perceived as being much closer to the Labour Party in Scotland with little change in this perception during the 1990s.

Table 4.3:   Perceptions of position of SNP, 1974-1997

	1974	1979	1992	1997
Closer to Conservatives	17	24	14	11
Closer to Labour	37	52	63	62
Neither/Equal/DK	46	24	23	27
N (=100%)	1175	729	957	852

Source: Scottish Election Surveys, 1974, 1979, 1992, 1997.

It may be this move to the left by the SNP that explains the distinctive values identified in the models in Table 4.2. First, the models of socialist-laissez faire values suggest that the difference between Scotland and the rest of Great Britain does not persist once the effect of national identity has been taken into account. This suggests that a feeling of 'Scottishness' goes along with left-wing values and suggests that the presence of the SNP has successfully linked Scottish nationalism to socialism in the value systems of the Scottish public. Table 4.4 provides further evidence to support this. It gives the position on each of the scales of groups of people defined by the national identity they chose, in Scotland and in England. (See Chapter Three for more detail on national identity measures.) The table shows that those respondents who expressed Scottishness over Britishness were more socialist in their values than those who adopted Britishness either equally to Scottishness or more than Scottishness. This relationship does not exist between socialist values and English identity. The other two scales do not show a clear relationship with national identity in Scotland.

This relationship between Scottishness and socialism provides an excellent example of the second source of social constraint identified by Converse (1964): that is the way that the elements of belief systems are diffused from elites to the mass public via 'packages' of systems. Thus, in Scotland the SNP have promoted both Scottish identity and left-wing values thereby creating a link between the two in the mass public. Other theories of the formation of mass public opinion support this interpretation:

> Many citizens ... pay too little attention to public affairs to be able to respond critically to the political communications they encounter; rather, they are blown about by whatever current information manages to develop the greatest intensity. (Zaller, 1992)

Scotland in the last 20 years has witnessed information supporting Scottish national identity and left-wing values reach a new intensity, and so it is unsurprising that mass political values should have moved in this direction.

Table   4.4:   National   identity   and   value   scales

	Scottish/ English not British	Scottish/ English more than British	Scottish/ English equal to British	British more than Scottish/ English	British not Scottish/ English
Socialist-Laissez Faire					
Scotland	13.62	14.17	15.37	15.77	15.60
England	15.12	15.86	15.51	16.07	15.65
Liberal-Authoritarian					
Scotland	18.63	18.42	19.07	16.79	17.95
England	20.24	19.20	19.02	18.40	18.73
Nationalist-Cosmopolitan					
Scotland	17.32	16.75	15.97	17.84	16.42
England	15.31	15.22	15.53	16.21	16.13
N					
Scotland	199	313	207	35	31
England	179	383	1073	338	202

Source: British Election Survey 1997.

Low values on the scales mean (respectively): more left-wing, more liberal, and more British nationalist.

Unfortunately it is not possible to construct the value scales for earlier periods in Scotland. Thus, Table 4.5 uses a proxy measure for the socialist-laissez faire scale – that is the questionnaire item 'Income and wealth should be redistributed to ordinary working people'. This question has been asked (albeit with small variations in wording) across the period 1974-1997. Table 4.5 summarises the position of Scotland and the rest of Great Britain on this issue by looking at the proportion within each area who agreed with the statement. If the above hypothesis is correct, we would expect to find that during the period 1974-1997 people in Scotland moved to the left on this issue. We might also hypothesise that in the rest of Great Britain there would be a move to the right during the 1980s (when the dominant political discourse was that of the Conservatives) and a subsequent move back to the left at the 1997 general election.

Table 4.5 provides weak evidence to support these hypotheses. We do indeed see a shift to the left in Scotland over this period from 58 per cent in 1974 to 69 per cent in 1997. Similarly, the rest of Britain appear to move slightly to the right, with a shift back to the left in 1997. However, the difficulties of using a single questionnaire item, which itself has changed over the period, have been described above, and whilst this evidence is in the predicted direction it does not provide a rigorous test of values in Scotland over the two decades.

Table 4.5:   **Attitudes to redistribution of wealth, 1974-1997**

	1974	1979	1992	1997
% agreeing				
Scotland	58	57	60	69
Rest of Great Britain	54	51	46	59
N (=100%)				
Scotland	1175	729	957	852
Rest of Great Britain	2157	1744	2577	2570

Source: British Election Surveys, 1974-1997.

See notes to Table 5.1 (Chapter Five).

DO VALUES INFLUENCE VOTING BEHAVIOUR?

Having seen that Scotland has distinctive value systems, we must now ask whether these values explain voting behaviour. Do positions on these scales translate into votes in the same way in Scotland and the rest of Britain? The relationship between vote and values is shown in Table 4.6, which shows the average position on each scale for each geographical area.

In terms of their positions on these scales, Conservative voters in Scotland and England are not different. However, Labour voters in Scotland are significantly more left-wing than their counterparts south of the border and also significantly less nationalistic (in their attitudes towards the British state). This seems to reinforce the findings above – that Scotland is not different on the liberal-authoritarian dimension but that the presence of the SNP has moved Labour voters as well as its own voters to the left and towards a less positive image of the British state. However, this does not take into account the different structure of social groups in the two areas, which we have already seen has a significant impact on these value systems in itself. We need to assess the impact of the value systems over and above differences of social structure. For example, it may be the case that Labour voters in Scotland are more left-wing than Labour voters in the rest of Great Britain because a greater proportion of Scottish Labour voters are from the working class, or live in accommodation that is rented from a local authority.

Table 4.6:   Vote and value scales

	Did not Vote	Conservative	Labour	Liberal Democrat	SNP
Socialist-Laissez Faire					
Scotland	14.56	19.12	13.16*	15.16	14.09
England	15.33	18.56	13.81	15.02	-
Liberal-Authoritarian					
Scotland	18.29	19.90	18.50	18.55	18.11
England	18.45	20.29	18.61	18.09	-
Nationalist-Cosmopolitan					
Scotland	16.57	14.84	16.84*	17.49	17.64
England	16.04	14.26	16.31	16.69	-
N					
Scotland	159	100	353	87	129
England	480	622	984	358	-

Source: British Election Survey 1997.

Low values on the scales mean (respectively): more left-wing, more liberal, and more British nationalist.

* indicates a statistically significant (at 5%) difference between Scotland and England among voters for the party concerned.

In order to assess the impact of these value scales on voting behaviour, we use logistic regression models of a series of binary outcome variables, the likelihood of voting Conservative, Labour or SNP. The results are in Table 4.7. In these models Conservative and Labour voting is measured across the whole of Great Britain, while models relating to the SNP are based on Scottish respondents only. The coefficients from three models are reported. Model I looks only at the coefficient for Scotland to assess if Scotland is different in its likelihood of voting Conservative or Labour. Here we see that in both cases Scotland is significantly different to the rest of Great Britain – being less likely to vote Conservative and more likely to vote Labour. Model II looks at the impact of the value scales on the likelihood of particular votes. There remains a significant deficit in Conservative voting in Scotland after having controlled for the value scales. Of the scales themselves, attitudes on all three are significant predictors of Conservative vote, whilst only position on the socialist-laissez faire scale is a significant predictor of Labour voting. The models also show that once value positions are taken into account, Scotland is no longer more supportive of the Labour Party than the rest of Great Britain – though we should note that given the four party competition in Scotland we might have expected Labour to do slightly worse in Scotland. This is especially true given that at recent elections the SNP have specifically targeted Labour voters. Thus, although there is no significant difference between Scotland and the rest of Great Britain, it is arguable that Labour do relatively better in Scotland given greater party competition.

Models testing for interactions between the positions on these scales and living in Scotland were also looked at but were found not to be significant. This suggests that the relationship between value positions and vote is the same in Scotland as elsewhere in Great Britain. The model of SNP voting shows that this is unrelated to left-right attitudes and to liberal-authoritarian attitudes; however it is significantly affected by attitudes to the British state.

The final model (Model III) adds in the structural and identity variables described above (see Table 4.2) to assess whether these relationships between vote and value scales persist after taking into account variability between social groups. The key finding from these

Table 4.7:   Models of voting behaviour

	Conservative	Labour	SNP
Model I			
Scotland	-0.92	0.16	NA
	(0.12)	(0.08)	
Model II			
Scotland	-0.83	-0.04	NA
	(0.16)	(0.10)	
Socialist-Laissez	0.36	-0.23	-0.02
Faire	(0.02)	(0.01)	(0.03)
Liberal-	0.14	-0.02	-0.02
Authoritarian	(0.02)	(0.01)	(0.03)
Nationalist-	-0.12	0.01	0.10
Cosmopolitan	(0.02)	(0.01)	(0.04)
Model III			
Scotland	-0.51	0.07	NA
	(0.27)	(0.19)	
Socialist-Laissez	0.33	-0.21	0.01
Faire	(0.02)	(0.02)	(0.04)
Liberal-	0.13	-0.04	-0.05
Authoritarian	(0.02)	(0.02)	(0.04)
Nationalist-	-0.12	0.01	0.15
Cosmopolitan	(0.02)	(0.02)	(0.04)
Other significant variables			
Social class	*		
Gender	*		
Tenure	*		
Education		*	
Religion	*	*	
Age		*	
Class identity	*	*	
National identity	*	*	*
N	3422	3422	852

Source: British Election Survey 1997.

* indicates that this variable had a significant coefficient in Model III (at 5 per cent level). Standard errors are in brackets.

models is that there is a significant Conservative voting deficit in Scotland even after the effects both of value systems and of social structure are taken into consideration. In addition to the coefficients for Scotland and for the value scales, the other variables which had a significant impact on the likelihood of voting for a party are indicated in the table. We can see that both Conservative and Labour voting are significantly related to structure and identity variables – over and above the relationship with value structures. However, in line with previous findings (Brand et al, 1993) the likelihood of voting SNP is related to national identity but not to other social structural variables. (It is worth noting here that this is not to say that SNP support is unrelated to social structure but rather that in predicting SNP support in Scotland we have to take into account the fact that the social demographic profile of SNP and Labour voters is very similar: this is discussed further in Chapter Seven.)

Thus, we need to find explanations as to why the Conservative vote in Scotland is so weak (and also why the Labour vote holds up even in the face of competition from the SNP). One possible explanation for these differences may be couched in terms of the 'political ethos' in Scotland.

POLITICAL ETHOS

As described above the political ethos of a society is related to the values held by the members of that society; it is also shaped by the dominant political discourses of the society. We have already mentioned how the SNP, and to some extent the Labour Party, have linked together Scottish nationalism and left-wing attitudes, so that within the mass public they now tend to go hand in hand. This may lead to a perception that to be right wing is, therefore, to be anti-Scottish. Thus, the relative unpopularity of the Conservative Party in Scotland may be due to their being viewed as anti-Scottish.

We can test this proposition by looking at the perception, or images, of the parties held by the public. In the Scottish Election Survey, respondents were asked to what extent they trusted the parties to work in Scotland's interest. The perceptions of the Conservative Party are shown in Table 4.8, separately for people who identify with each of the four parties. (Perceptions of other parties are discussed in Chapter Seven.)

Amongst non-Conservative identifiers, over 90 per cent of respondents expected that the Conservative Party would work in Scotland's interest 'only some of the time' or 'almost never'. However, more strikingly, over half of even Conservative identifiers also expected the Conservatives to work in Scotland's interest only some of the time or almost never. In stark contrast, among other party identifiers over 70 per cent expected their own party to work in Scotland's interest either 'just about always' or 'most of the time' (details not shown in the table).

Table 4.8:   Trust Conservatives to work in Scotland's interest by party identity

	party identity				
	Con	Lab	Lib Dem	SNP	All
Just about always	7	0	0	2	2
Most of the time	37	2	5	2	9
Only some of the time	42	33	60	23	36
Almost never	13	63	36	73	52
Don't know	2	3	0	1	2
N (=100%)	140	397	90	140	767

Source: Scottish Election Survey 1997.

CONCLUSION

What then does this tell us about the 'political ethos' of Scotland and how might it influence the future development of Scottish politics? The main conclusion to be drawn from the analysis we have presented is the way in which elite political discourse shapes mass opinion. The deliberate linking of nationalist and left-wing values by both the SNP and the Labour Party in Scotland have led to a linkage of these two dimension in the political ethos of the society. This leads to a situation in which to say one is Scottish is also to say one has left-wing views, and conversely to say that one is British, rather than Scottish, is to assert right-wing views. No such link between these dimensions is visible in the rest of Great Britain and it is this linkage which explains Scottish distinctiveness.

Thus, the Conservatives in Scotland are viewed negatively not only because of their policy positions (see Chapter Five) or their political values in the broad sense. Rather they are viewed negatively because they are perceived as anti-Scottish. The establishment of the Scottish Parliament in 1999 will no doubt have a further impact on this framework. On the one hand, we might speculate that this will serve to reinforce the dominant discourse of nationalist and socialist values, which would further harm the Conservatives in Scotland. However an alternative possibility exists, whereby the Conservatives find a way of working within the framework of the Parliament to regain their 'Scottish' credentials and to begin to unpick the relationship between Scottishness and socialism. We return to a fuller discussion of these prospects in Chapter Seven.

5

Policy Preferences

INTRODUCTION

There are four particular reasons to analyse Scottish policy preferences as distinct from the political values which we looked at in Chapter Four. The first is that policy is the practical effect of values. Thus when people place themselves on a scale running from left to right, the practical political effect of that will be to influence their attitudes to such policy areas as redistributing wealth or supporting comprehensive education. Scales of values may give more consistent measures of attitudes (Evans et al, 1996), but they do not give us answers to how people judge more immediate questions of current policy. In any case, testing that the patterns detected for value scales can also be found in attitudes to distinct items of policy tends to validate the scales themselves, because it grounds them in practical politics.

That, in fact, is the second point: debate about individual policies is what politics purports to be all about. Values do, of course, underlie attitudes to policy, but, in the end, what counts is the policies themselves. Thus, although the Labour Party may have undertaken its policy review between 1992 and 1997 in order to bring itself closer to the values of the British electorate (Butler and Kavanagh, 1997; Heath et al, 1994), the end result is a set of policies which it is now putting in place. Any academic analysis which failed to look at policies themselves – and studied only values – would be failing to address the actual discourses of politicians and of everyday discussions of politics.

Nowhere is this more true than in the debate about Scottish politics in the UK – the third reason to be interested in policy. As we will see in the next chapter, the main reason why people supported the setting up of a Scottish Parliament in the referendum of September 1997 was that they had clear expectations of what it would do in particular areas of policy. That is hardly surprising, because the whole tenor of the debate about Scottish political distinctiveness over the last two or three decades has been principally about disagreements over policy, and the main argument for a Scottish Parliament is that it will produce better policy, by which is usually meant policies more in keeping with what people want in Scotland (Paterson, 1998b). However, although the debate has been about putative policy differences between Scotland and the rest of Britain, what these are and what their implications are have been more open to dispute. It has frequently been claimed, for example, that Scotland is more left-wing than England and therefore is more likely to support more nationalisation of industry, more redistribution of wealth, a more egalitarian education system, and so on. And yet there is evidence that, on many policies, Scotland is not all that different from England (Brown et al, 1998; Curtice, 1996). Partly because of the strength of the assumption that the Scots do favour different types of policies – and partly because Scotland has a four-party system in which the Conservatives are at best the third-largest – the political parties in Scotland tend to occupy rather different policy positions from those they occupy in England. So it is possible that the relationship between people's policy preferences and their voting practices could be different in Scotland and England. For example, in the general election of May 1997, people in Scotland who favoured higher taxes in order to finance higher public spending had the choice of two parties (SNP and Liberal Democrats), rather than just one as in England.

Thus, in all these respects, the whole topic of distinctive Scottish policy preferences raises questions about the relationship between national identity and policy, in the same way as did the question of political values in Chapter Four. If Scotland does indeed favour more left-wing policies than England, is that because Scotland is more working-class or because being more left-wing has become a badge of Scottish identity? We saw in Chapter Four that Scotland was indeed rather more left-wing than England, and that this was related to national identity. But how consistent are people when they translate this set of national political values into preferences among policies?

Whether the new Parliament in Scotland will satisfy Scots' desire for distinct policies will depend partly on whether it will have control of the relevant policy areas – the fourth reason for being interested in Scots policy preferences. Are Scots distinctive mainly on the topics which will be transferred to the Parliament? Put differently: has the Labour government (with the support of the Scottish political establishment) chosen correctly when deciding the balance between powers for the Parliament and powers reserved to Westminster? If it has, then we might expect the Parliament to have quite harmonious relations with Westminster, at least so long as the Westminster government is well-disposed towards decentralisation of policy making. If the balance is wrong, however, we might expect tensions, which could result in sizable shifts of Scottish votes towards the SNP and other parties which favour a stronger Parliament than the one that will be set up in 1999.

This chapter looks at Scottish policy preferences in two main ways. First it asks the central question: is Scotland different? To the extent that it is, the next task is to explain why. And then there is the question of whether Scotland is now more different than it was in the 1970s (when British politics seemed still to be fairly homogeneous, and when support for a Scottish Parliament was less emphatic than it was in 1997).

The chapter, second, looks at the effects of Scottish policy preferences on voting. Can the unpopularity of the Conservatives in Scotland be explained by any distinctiveness in Scottish attitudes to policy? Is the relationship between policy preferences and voting the same in Scotland as in the rest of Britain? Is voting SNP strongly tied to specific policy preferences?

IS SCOTLAND DIFFERENT?

The British Election Survey can be used to compare Scotland with the rest of Britain on many individual policy areas. A broad selection of these is summarised in Table 5.1, comparing Scotland with England and with Wales. Also noted there is the result of simple tests of

Table 5.1:   **Policy preferences in the nations of Britain**

	England	Wales	Scotland	
Government should put more money into the NHS[1]	95	96	96	
Government should encourage the growth of private medicine[1]	31	29	27	
Government should spend more money on education[1]	93	95	95	
Government should get rid of private education in Britain[1]	19	24	29	**
The cleverest children should be selected for education in separate schools[2]	49	32	27	**
It is a good thing for schools to be made to compete against each other for pupils[2]	31	24	24	
People who break the law should be given stiffer sentences[2]	84	86	83	
Life sentences should mean life[2]	87	91	87	
Prisons should try harder to reform prisoners rather than just punishing them[2]	77	74	78	
People should be allowed to use their cars as much as they like, even if it causes damage to the environment[2]	23	29	26	
For the sake of the environment, car users should pay higher taxes[2]	29	17	24	
Income and wealth should be redistributed towards ordinary working people[2]	58	73	69	**
Government should spend more money to get rid of poverty[1]	90	95	94	*

[Table 5.1 continued on next page]

[Table 5.1 continued]

	England	Wales	Scotland	
It would be better if everyone paid less tax and had to pay more towards their own health care, schools and the like[2]	17	12	14	
Taxes should be as low as possible, and people should have to provide more for themselves even if it means that some people suffer[2]	8	9	6	
Everyone's taxes should go up to provide better old age pensions for all[2]	49	54	57	
Government should increase taxes and spend more on health, education and social benefits[3]	71	66	73	
Government should introduce stricter laws to regulate the activities of trade unions[1]	35	31	32	
Government should give workers more say in running the places where they work[1]	73	78	74	
The British government should sign up to the Social Chapter so that British workers have the same rights at work as everyone else in Europe[4]	39	42	44	*
The law should set a minimum wage so that no employer can pay their workers too little[5]	67	74	76	*
There should be more nationalisation of companies by government[6]	26	39	35	[*]
Government should spend less on defence[1]	54	52	63	
Government should give more aid to poor countries in Africa and Asia[2]	31	31	35	
N (= 100%)	2397	173	852	

[Notes for Table 5.1 are on the next page]

Notes for Table 5.1:

Source: British Election Survey 1997.

Last column indicates levels of significance: Scotland different from rest of Britain at 1% (**), 5% (*) or 10% ([*]) level of significance in a loglinear model (using full set of response categories, not only the one shown in the Table).

Notes on coding of response categories:

[1] *percentage choosing 'definitely should' or 'probably should' (other categories being 'doesn't matter either way', 'probably should not' and 'definitely should not').*

[2] *percentage choosing 'agree strongly' or 'agree' (other categories being 'neither agree nor disagree', 'disagree' and 'disagree strongly').*

[3] *The options offered against this were 'Government should reduce taxes and spend less on health, education and social benefits' and 'Government should keep taxes and spending at the same level as now'.*

[4] *The option offered against this was 'The British government should not sign up to the Social Chapter because it would cost too many British workers their jobs'.*

[5] *The option offered against this was 'There should be no minimum wage because a minimum wage set by law would cost too many low paid workers their jobs'.*

[6] *The options offered against this were 'There should be more privatisation of companies by government' and 'Things should be left as they are now'.*

statistical significance to assess whether there is any evidence that Scotland is different; these tests (based on a loglinear model) used the full set of response categories, unlike the condensed versions which have been shown for most of the variables in the table. The general first impression is of remarkable uniformity across the nations of Britain. In most areas of policy, Scotland is not notably different from England or Wales: differences relate to intensity of feeling rather than to direction, so that, in almost every case where there is a clear Scottish majority for some position, there is also a majority in England and Wales (the only exception being attitudes to selective schools, to which we return below). Moreover, this similarity is not because the claim that Scotland is left-of-centre is manifestly untrue: it is because, in most of these policy areas, the whole of Britain remains a broadly social democratic place, despite 18 years of a firmly right-wing Conservative government (see also Heath and Park, 1997). The same is true of issues which cannot be readily placed on a left-right scale. Thus, also from Table 5.1, Scotland's attitudes to car use are similar to those in England and Wales. It shows little sign of being more lenient on criminals, and it shares the general British view that, once in prison, criminals should be reformed as much as punished. And it is not notably more internationalist than the rest of Britain, as the question on aid to the developing world shows.

Nevertheless, there are some topics on which there is fairly clear evidence that the intensity of Scottish feeling does differ, and several of these relate to the core of the debate about the future of the welfare state. Thus Scots are more likely than people in England to favour government action to end poverty or to redistribute wealth. They also are more likely to favour a statutory minimum wage. The Scots probably remain more friendly to state ownership of industry. And they are more in favour of Britain's signing up to the European Union's Social Chapter (which the Labour government did on taking office).

It has to be said, though, that these differences are still quite small in absolute terms: statistical significance tells us only about the strength of evidence for a difference, not about the strength of the difference in real political terms. However, that could not be said of the most striking differences of all, on two of the questions relating to education. Scots are much more likely than people elsewhere in Britain to oppose selection for secondary school, and they are more hostile to the private sector in education. This finding has been noted frequently elsewhere: it is the area of social policy in which Scots have had the most clearly distinctive attitudes for some time (Paterson, 1997).

Generally, these differences between Scotland and England as a whole are seen even when we compare Scotland with individual English regions (details not shown in the tables): of the items which show Scotland as different from England, Scotland is also different from the most left-wing parts of England (the north, usually) on redistribution, nationalisation, private education, and selective education. But on all the topics other than the educational ones, Scotland is similar to Wales.

So there are policy differences, large enough to sustain a different debate in Scotland. The striking point, though, is that – with the exception of education – the differences are not mainly in areas which will be within the powers of the Scottish Parliament. They mainly concern the overall structure of taxation, large-scale redistribution, and even some areas of foreign affairs. Of course, it could be that, when the Parliament is established, it itself will start to provoke different attitudes to policy in the topics for which it will be responsible. Nevertheless, at this stage, the argument that the Parliament will address just those areas where Scots want to be distinctive is not easily tenable.

WHY IS SCOTLAND DIFFERENT?

To the extent that Scotland does have distinctive policy positions, why is this so? There are two competing explanations, parallel to those which we looked at for political values in Chapter Four. One suggests that Scotland is different because it is structurally different (more working class etc). A refinement of this is that it is different because it has a different attitude to social structure (more people identifying themselves as working class). The other explanation is that it is different for reasons of national identity: in other words, even when we compare two people with similar social locations, the Scottish person will be more left wing than the English one simply because nationality confers a tendency to favour certain policy positions. The most obvious example might be in education: because education is at the heart of the debate about Scottish identity, we might expect people to associate their attitudes to Scottishness with their attitudes to Scottish education.

To test this, the policy variables in which Scotland was found to be different from England were modelled using logistic regression on the condensed versions of the variables as shown in Table 5.1. (Logistic regression is explained in the Appendix.) The key explanatory variable is the one which compares Scotland with the rest of Britain, and it is this which is shown in Table 5.2 for each of four

Table 5.2: Scotland difference in models of policy preference

	model			
dependent variable	I	II	III	IV
get rid of private education	0.28 (0.07)	0.24 (0.08)	0.23 (0.08)	0.19 (0.13)
clever children in separate schools	-0.40 (0.08)	-0.39 (0.08)	-0.39 (0.08)	-0.45 (0.13)
redistribute wealth	0.21 (0.07)	0.17 (0.08)	0.15 (0.08)	0.15 (0.12)
get rid of poverty	0.26 (0.14)	0.29 (0.16)	0.28 (0.16)	0.12 (0.22)
EU Social Chapter	0.11 (0.07)	0.09 (0.07)	0.08 (0.07)	0.22 (0.12)
minimum wage	0.18 (0.07)	0.16 (0.07)	0.15 (0.07)	0.02 (0.11)
nationalisation	0.17 (0.07)	0.08 (0.08)	0.07 (0.08)	0.08 (0.12)

Source: British Election Survey 1997.

The table shows the regression coefficient (and its standard error) for the dichotomous variable denoting Scotland in multiple logistic regressions as set out below.

The names of the dependent variables have been simplified: see Table 5.1 for full versions. In the regressions, they have been coded as implied by the percentages in Table 5.1.

Key to models:

I   Scotland variable only.

II Add social structure (sex, age, class, housing tenure, education).

III Add self-assigned social class.

IV Add national identity (European, British, English, Welsh, Irish, Northern Irish, Scottish, other).

models. For all the variables apart from the one recording attitudes to selective schooling, the coefficient of this variable is positive when Scotland is more left-wing than the rest of Britain.

In the first model, the 'Scotland' indicator is the only explanatory variable, and so these coefficients simply confirm the findings reported above that Scotland is more left-wing on all these variables. (The statistical significance is sometimes less than in Table 5.1 because a condensed version of the dependent variables was used in Table 5.2.) The second model controls for social structure – social class (Hope-Goldthorpe classes), sex, housing tenure, age, and educational level. The third model controls also for attitude to social structure, by including a variable for self-assigned class: that is, did the respondent think of himself or herself as working class? The fourth model further controls for national identity, by including the variables which recorded whether the respondent felt European, British, English, Welsh, Irish, Northern Irish, Scottish, or other nationality (as in Chapter Four).

Comparing the second model in the table with the first, we can see that the addition of social-structural variables made almost no difference to the size of the Scotland coefficient, except on the variable recording attitudes to nationalisation. Thus, as for the analysis of values in Chapter Four, social structure mostly does not explain Scotland's different position on policy, but it does explain it for nationalisation: that is, Scotland is more in favour of nationalisation simply because Scotland contains more of those social groups which tend to be more in favour of nationalisation. For example, we saw in Table 5.1 that 35 per cent of Scots but only 26 per cent of the English favoured more nationalisation. But that difference is explained partly by the fact that people who rent their homes from local authorities are more likely to favour nationalisation, and Scotland has more such people: thus, if we look only at this group, the proportions in favour of more nationalisation were 39 per cent in both Scotland and the rest of Britain. The rest of the explanation is in terms of social class. Scotland has slightly more skilled workers, and slightly fewer professional workers, than the rest of Britain, and thus has a class structure that is more favourably disposed towards nationalisation. If we look only at blue collar workers, we find that the proportions in favour of more nationalisation were 33 per cent in Scotland and 36 per cent in the rest of Britain (not a statistically significant difference); similarly, if we look only at high-status professional people, we find that the proportions in favour of more nationalisation were 19 per cent in Scotland and 21 per cent the rest of Britain also (not a statistically significant difference).

No further change in the Scotland coefficients comes about after self-assigned class is added (the third model of Table 5.2): thus the explanation of the differences in attitudes to policy is not found in different attitudes to the social structure. But on four of the policy variables, the statistical significance of the Scotland variables drops substantially after the measures of national identity are included (fourth model). Thus – comparing models I and IV – we see that national identity can explain distinct Scottish attitudes to government action on poverty, to private education, to redistribution of wealth, to the minimum wage. This is also, to some extent, true of attitudes to the European Union's Social Chapter. The only policy variable on which national identity makes almost no impact is attitudes to selective schooling, where the Scotland variable remains almost as statistically significant in model IV as in model I.

The pattern of these associations with national identity is illustrated in Table 5.3 which shows the views of people who did or did not identify themselves as Scottish. (The two per cent of people elsewhere in Britain who identified themselves as Scottish have been excluded from this analysis because they do not provide a statistically reliable base for comparison.) In all cases except for attitudes to the EU Social Chapter, the non-Scottish identifiers in Scotland lay in between the non-Scottish identifiers in the rest of Britain and the Scottish identifiers in Scotland. Indeed, the non-Scottish identifiers in Scotland were more or less the same as non-Scottish identifiers in the rest of Britain on attitudes to government action to get rid of poverty, on redistribution of wealth and on the minimum wage.

So, insofar as Scotland does have different policy preferences from the rest of Britain, it is largely (although not wholly) because certain aspects of policy have become closely linked to feelings about Scottish national identity. The conclusion is thus similar to that in Chapter Four on political values.

Table   5.3:   Scottish policy preferences compared to rest of Britain by whether people consider themselves   to   be   Scottish

	rest of Britain (not 'Scottish')	Scotland (not 'Scottish')	Scotland ('Scottish')
get rid of private education	19	25	30
clever children in separate schools	47	34	25
redistribute wealth	59	58	72
get rid of poverty	90	91	95
EU Social Chapter	39	48	42
minimum wage	67	69	77
nationalisation	27	34	35
N (=100%)	2501	174	678

Source: British Election Survey 1997.

Coding of response categories is the same as in Table 5.1.

HOW HAVE SCOTTISH POLICY PREFERENCES CHANGED?

One explanation that has been given of developments in Scottish politics in the last few years is that it has been a response to the period of Conservative government in which the Scottish majority was not reflected in the majority at Westminster. The starkest version of that claim is that Scotland moved left while England moved firmly to the right.

Assessing this is made difficult by the absence of directly comparable measures in appropriate surveys. However, the British Election Surveys of October 1974, 1979, 1987, 1992 and 1997 did contain broadly comparable questions on government funding of the National Health Service, on government action to eradicate poverty, on redistribution of wealth, on giving workers more say in industry, and on aid to the developing world. This group of five variables fortunately includes some on which – as we have seen – there was

Scottish distinctiveness in 1997, and some on which there was none. Comparable questions on education were not so readily available (partly because there were large policy changes in this topic during the period), but an approximate comparison can be obtained for 1974, 1979 and 1997 by using a question about comprehensive education in the earlier years alongside the 1997 question about selective education. All the comparisons should be treated with caution because of the differences in question wording.

Summary results are in Table 5.4 (the section on redistribution has already been shown in Table 4.5). The main point to note is that the whole of Britain moved steadily to the left in attitudes to the NHS, to poverty, to redistribution, and to workers' say in industry. In nearly every respect, Scotland simply followed this trend. There was no change in attitudes to aid for the developing world, either in Scotland or in the rest of Britain. Only in relation to comprehensive education was there a clear divergence between Scotland and the rest of Britain. This could be explained by the generally more satisfactory experience of comprehensive education in Scotland than elsewhere (Benn and Chitty, 1996), but we must also bear in mind that the 1997 survey question here differed quite a lot from the 1974 and 1979 versions.

So the Conservatives were remarkably unsuccessful in shifting popular attitudes to policy, a point which has been made in more detail for Britain as a whole in the 1980s and 1990s by Heath and Park (1997). The left-of-centre policy preferences of the Scots were not the outcome of a unique social evolution in the last two decades, except possibly in a limited number of high-profile topics such as education and growing poverty. The evolution was shared with the rest of Britain, but the political reactions to it differed. It is to these that we now turn.

EFFECTS OF POLICY PREFERENCES ON VOTING

As we noted in Chapter One – and as has been widely discussed – voting patterns in Scotland became increasingly distinct during the 1980s and 1990s. The hostility of Scots to the Conservative Party was often described in political debate as an hostility to Conservative policies. To what extent can this be explained by Scotland's distinctive policy preferences? Are these policy preferences distinct

Table 5.4: **Trends in policy preferences, Scotland compared to the rest of Britain, 1974-1997**

	1974	1979	1987	1992	1997
increased government spending on NHS					
Scotland	87	90	93	96	96
rest of Britain	84	87	90	92	95
comprehensive education					
Scotland	37	31	NA	NA	56
rest of Britain	39	31	NA	NA	37
redistribution of wealth					
Scotland	58	57	64	60	69
rest of Britain	54	51	49	46	59
government spending to eradicate poverty					
Scotland	83	83	89	94	94
rest of Britain	85	80	86	92	90
workers more say in workplace					
Scotland	59	49	76	78	74
rest of Britain	57	55	76	76	74
more aid to developing world					
Scotland	39	36	38	41	35
rest of Britain	39	36	38	36	31
N (=100%)					
Scotland	1175	149	366	957	852
rest of Britain	2157	1744	3460	2577	2570

[Notes for Table 5.4 are on the next page]

Notes for Table 5.4:

Source: British Election Surveys 1974, 1979, 1987, 1992, 1997.

Note on coding of response categories:

1997, 1992 and 1987: response categories are explained in the note to Table 5.1.

1979 and 1974: all the response categories were 'very important to do ...', 'fairly important to do ...', 'doesn't matter', 'fairly important not to do ...' and 'very important not to do ...'; the first two have been equated to the first two in 1997 and 1992 (i.e. either to 'definitely should' and 'probably should' or to 'strongly agree' and 'agree').

The question on comprehensive education in 1974 and 1979 asked if the government should establish comprehensives. In 1987 and 1992 there was no question on comprehensive or selective education (denoted by NA in the table). In 1997, the question used here was the one on selective education shown in Table 5.1, but with the response categories reversed to make them comparable to the earlier years.

enough to account for such deep unpopularity as the Conservatives encountered? Even where policy preferences are similar in Scotland and the rest of Britain, are their effects on voting the same? And have the effects of policy preferences changed since the 1970s?

The other most notable feature of Scottish party politics is the strength of the Scottish National Party. Do its voters and sympathisers express any distinctive attitudes to policy? This question will become increasingly important after the Scottish Parliament is set up, because the main party conflict there will probably be between the SNP and the Labour Party.

Table 5.5 summarises the relationship between policy variables and vote in 1997 in separate multiple logistic regressions for Conservative vote, Labour vote (both across the whole of Britain) and SNP vote (Scotland only). (The full set of variables which were tested for inclusion were those shown in Table 5.1 and their interactions with the Scotland indicator.) For Conservative and Labour voting,

Table 5.5: **Associations between policy preferences and voting**

	party		
Conservative vote (all Britain)	Labour vote (all Britain)	SNP (Scotland)	
		vote	vote or second preference
	+government spending on NHS		
government spending on education			
get rid of private education	get rid of private education		
+clever children in separate schools			clever children in separate schools
	stiffer sentences		
life should mean life			
higher car taxes			
+redistribute wealth	+redistribute wealth		redistribute wealth
get rid of poverty	get rid of poverty		
		raise taxes for pensions	
+higher taxes and spending		higher taxes and spending	higher taxes and spending
stricter trade union laws	+stricter trade union laws		
			more say for workers
+EU Social Chapter	+EU Social Chapter		
minimum wage	+minimum wage		
nationalisation	nationalisation		nationalisation
+defence cuts		defence cuts	
			aid to developing world
Scotland			

[Notes for Table 5.5 are on the next page]

Notes for Table 5.5:

Source: British Election Surveys 1997.

The table shows only those policy variables which were associated with at least one of the types of voting. The full set of variables which was tested for inclusion was those shown in Table 5.1 and their interactions with the Scotland indicator. The direction of association is discussed in the text.

[+] Also significant in an analysis confined to the Scottish sample only: see text for explanation.

The names of the dependent variables have been simplified: see Table 5.1 for full versions.

almost all the variables had the expected effect, even in this multiple regression. The more left-wing were people's views about policy, the less likely were they to vote Conservative and the more likely to vote Labour; the only slightly surprising result is that favouring stronger jail sentences for criminals makes people more likely to vote Labour than otherwise.

For our purposes, the important points have to do with Scottish distinctiveness. On Conservative voting, the party has a Scottish deficit even after taking account of all the policy variables. Further modelling showed that the deficit cannot be explained, either, by these policy variables' having a different effect on Conservative voting in Scotland: for example, favouring redistribution of wealth has the same effect on the propensity to vote Conservative in Scotland as in the rest of Britain. The deficit is also not amenable to explanation as a growing hostility to the Conservatives during the 1980s and 1990s. For example, in the 1974 election survey, the proportions of the whole sample (including non-voters) supporting the Conservatives were 21 per cent in Scotland and 31 per cent in the rest of Britain, a gap of ten per cent. In 1997, they were 11 per cent and 24 per cent, a gap of 13 per cent. (This comparison is not statistically significant in the logistic model.) This fairly constant Scottish effect can be contrasted with some of the policy variables, which did show a different relationship with Conservative voting in 1997 compared to

1974. Being in favour of more government spending on the NHS or on eradicating poverty, and supporting more workers' say in industry, more sharply differentiated non-Conservative from Conservative voters in 1997 than they had done in 1974. But that change, too, was the same in Scotland as in the rest of Britain.

So Scotland's hostility to the Conservatives cannot be fully explained by Scotland's having policy preferences which are at odds with the Conservatives', or in these policy preferences having a different effect in Scotland. It cannot be explained by a possibly ephemeral reaction to 18 years of Conservative government, because it was present in 1974 as well. Unlike Scottish distinctiveness on policy (and on values) it was not even amenable to explanation in terms of identity: a further model showed that the simple fact of living in Scotland was more strongly associated with Conservative vote than identifying as Scottish. (This point is discussed further in Chapter Six, where we relate it to the Conservatives' opposition to setting up a Scottish Parliament.) The Conservatives' unpopularity is more deep-seated than that, and represents a fundamental alienation of the party from Scottish society as a whole. These conclusions in terms of policy are very similar to the conclusions we reached in Chapter Four in terms of political values (Table 4.7).

Labour, by contrast, has done well in Scotland, but largely because it has benefited disproportionately from the electoral system. As we saw in Chapter Three, its Scottish share of the vote in 1997 was not much greater than its share in the rest of Britain, even before the distinctive Scottish policy preferences are taken into account. Thus the policy variables which influence Labour voting were the same in Scotland as in the rest of Britain (and are shown in Table 5.5). So the conclusion for Labour is rather the opposite to the conclusion for the Conservatives. Whereas Conservative unpopularity could not be explained by anything other than a deep alienation from Scottish society, Labour popularity cannot be explained by any particular affinity with Scotland. Again, the conclusion is similar to that reached in terms of political values in Chapter Four.

In the medium term, that could cause problems for Labour, as it comes to find that its main political opponent in the Scottish Parliament is the SNP. Table 5.5 shows that, compared to voting for the Conservative and Labour Parties, SNP voting is not clearly related to most of the policy variables. Although that is partly because the Scottish sample size is smaller than the British one on which the analysis of Conservative and Labour voting can be based, even when the analysis of these parties' vote is also confined to the Scottish sample, we still find that their support seems to be influenced by more policy variables than is support for the SNP: this is indicated by the crosses marked against variables in the table. This parallels the finding in Chapter Four that SNP support was not clearly related to political values on the socialist-laissez faire or the libertarian-authoritarian scales.

But, on those policy variables which do show an effect on SNP support, the party was competing for the same policy positions as the Labour Party – essentially, mainstream social democracy. This was even more clearly true of the pool of people who either were voting SNP or were willing to give the SNP as their second choice (43 per cent of the whole sample): they were clearly on the left politically: see the last column of Table 5.5. The point was confirmed further by modelling the difference between SNP and Labour voting among people who voted for one or other of these parties (details not shown in the Tables): although several policy variables helped to explain the choice as between these parties, none of them placed either party clearly to the left of the other. For example, SNP voters were more left-wing than Labour voters in opposition to stricter laws regulating the activities of trades unions and in support for defence cuts. Labour voters were more left wing than SNP voters in support for a minimum wage. Labour voters were more firmly in favour of stiffer sentences for criminals than were SNP voters.

We discuss the implications of this for the future contest between Labour and the SNP in Chapter Seven (and, in particular, we look in more detail at these differences in policy preferences among groups of party supporters in Table 7.7). The main point to note here is that the general election vote for Scotland's most distinctively Scottish political party owed only a limited amount to any distinctive Scottish policy preferences, partly because there are not many of these in the first place, and partly because – with the exception of attitudes to education and to redistribution – the SNP seems not yet to have created for itself a position on policy that can be a reason for people giving the party their support. Nevertheless, there is evidence that the party was beginning to create such a distinctive position among people who would consider voting for it even though they did not do so in 1997.

CONCLUSION

The main conclusion from this chapter is that Scottish policy preferences are not very distinct from those in the rest of Britain. Insofar as there are differences, however, they do put Scotland more to the left politically than elsewhere. These differences mostly cannot be explained by Scotland's having a different social structure to the rest of Britain: they are due, probably, to links between certain policy positions and Scottish national identity. A similar explanation in terms of identity can be given of the Conservative Party's deep and long-lasting unpopularity in Scotland.

In that sense, the limited evidence that Scotland does have distinct policy preferences could be taken to vindicate the setting up of a Scottish Parliament. But, with the exception of education, Scottish distinctiveness does not relate to the policy areas which will be transferred to the Parliament: it has more to do with the redistributive policies of social democracy. Since, further, the reason for the Labour Party's electoral success in Scotland seems to owe little to its having responded in any particularly distinctive way to Scottish policy concerns, these conclusions suggest that Scottish politics are unlikely to settle down tidily after the Scottish Parliament is elected in 1999. Scottish distinctiveness on policy will tend to press the Parliament beyond the powers which it will have initially, and the battle between the SNP and Labour for the leadership of the left-of-centre majority will ensure that the possibility of extending these powers will not go away.

We return to discuss the future of Scottish politics in Chapter Seven. Next, in Chapter Six, however, we examine the role which attitudes to policy, to parties, and to national identity played in the 1997 referendum which ensured that a Parliament will indeed be set up.

6

The Scottish Parliament

INTRODUCTION

In the run-up to the general election the Labour Party had promised Scotland a referendum on the establishment of a Parliament and, shortly after taking over government, passed legislation allowing the referendum to take place. Held on the 11 September 1997, the referendum asked people in Scotland to vote on two issues: whether or not a Parliament should be established and whether a Parliament should have tax varying powers. Scotland awoke on the 12 September to the news that the people had supported both propositions by impressive majorities.

In this chapter we deal with two main aspects of the debate about a Scottish Parliament. The first is to examine three competing explanations of voting behaviour and assess how well they explain the result in the referendum of 11 September. One of these explanations is a model of voting based on rational choice theory, the second is a claim that social location (for example, social class) can explain voting patterns, and the third is a model based on vote as an expression of national identity. We argue that understanding the vote in the referendum requires a model based not on economic rationality or on national identity but rather on welfare rationality. That is, people in Scotland voted for a Parliament with tax varying powers because they believed it would bring benefits to Scotland in terms of social welfare.

The second aspect of the debate is to consider the role which the issue of a Scottish Parliament played in the general election. In 1992, the Conservatives claimed that their defence of the constitutional status quo was a reason why their vote held up, and yet, in 1997 with the same policy, they lost all their seats in Scotland and a third of their remaining vote. Was the issue of a Scottish Parliament a factor in this collapse?

We focus primarily here on the question of how people intended to vote in the referendum. The survey questionnaire contained two questions aimed at mimicking the referendum questions. These were:

There are proposals to hold a referendum in Scotland to find out whether people want a Scottish Parliament to be set up. In such a referendum – supposing you had to vote 'Yes' or 'No' to the following questions – how would you vote?

Should there be a Scottish Parliament within the UK?

1 Yes
2 No
3 (Would not vote in referendum)
4 Other answer (WRITE IN)

Should a Scottish Parliament be able to increase or decrease income tax within a limit of three pence in the pound?

1 Yes
2 No
3 (Would not vote in referendum)
4 Other answer (WRITE IN)

Table 6.1 shows how respondents to the 1997 Scottish Election Study answered these questions. This table suggests that many Scots had decided on their referendum voting intention well in advance of both the general election and the announcement of the referendum itself; even opinion polls carried out well before the general election could predict the outcome of the referendum accurately. In addition, Table 6.1 shows that the Scottish Election Study, whilst still looking at *intended* vote, was remarkably close to the actual result. This is probably less surprising when we consider that the fieldwork for the survey was carried out during the period of the referendum campaign.

Table 6.1: Intended vote in referendum on Scottish Parliament

	May-Aug '96 (poll average)	Nov '96 (System 3)	Scottish Election Survey 1997	Result
Parliament				
Yes	63	70	72	74.3
No	26	21	21	25.7
Don't Know/ Not answered	11	8	7	
Tax-varying powers				
Yes	53	59	63	63.5
No	31	30	26	36.5
Don't Know/ Not answered	16	11	11	

In this chapter the questions above, on how people intended to vote on the two referendum questions, have been collapsed to give a five-fold measurement of intended referendum vote – Yes-Yes, Yes-No, No-No, No-Yes and Other (which includes all those who were undecided or said they would not vote on either question). By collapsing the questions in this way we are able to look at the likelihood of people choosing different combinations of vote intention. The proportions in these categories were 58 per cent Yes-Yes, ten per cent Yes-No, 16 per cent No-No, four per cent No-Yes, and 12 per cent other.

MODELS OF VOTING IN THE REFERENDUM

The models of voting used in this chapter were developed in the context of voting behaviour at general and local elections, at which the electorate are asked to choose among parties offering differing bundles of policy promises. As referendums are relatively infrequent and often assumed to be 'one-off' events there are no general models of referendum voting on which to draw. It is usually assumed that vote in a referendum is a simple expression of policy preference. However, this is not necessarily the case, and in the Scottish referendum is certainly misleading. In referendums voters are offered clear choices among preferences but not all the possible positions are offered. For example, in the Scottish referendum, independence from the UK state was not an option. Thus, in trying to understand the processes at work in people's decisions as to how to cast their vote at these referendums, we must look for explanations beyond a simple expression of policy preference.

Models based on rational choice theory, on the social location of voters in Scotland and on national identity have all been used to explain the distinctive pattern of voting in Scotland at general elections (Brand et al, 1993; Brand et al, 1994; Brown et al, 1996). This chapter applies each of these models in turn to voting intention in the referendum.

Rationality and the Referendum Vote

Models of voting behaviour based on rational choice theory have become commonplace in recent years, both in academic circles and in the common-sense explanations of election results. Beginning in the 1970s, political commentators identified a 'decade of dealignment' (Sarlvik and Crewe, 1983) during which, it was argued, voters became loosened from the anchors of social location and identity, and started to choose parties on the basis of rational decisions. Several models of these rational decisions have been put forward. The earliest of these was the 'issue voting' model (Downs, 1957; Sarlvik and Crewe, 1983), in which voters line up their own attitudes and preferences against the policy positions of the parties and cast their vote for the party closest to their own choices. This model has proved difficult to test and substantiate at the level of vote in a general election as the level of knowledge of party positions among the electorate is often quite low. Moreover, the issue voting model is not appropriate for modelling vote at a referendum, when the electorate are asked to state their own position on a single issue and not to choose from bundles of policy positions put forward by parties.

More recent models of voting, based on rational choice theory, have focused on the economic evaluations voters make. These models can be divided into two types (following Kinder and Kiewit, 1981), egocentric models and sociotropic models. The first of these, egocentric models, are based on economic evaluations of the voter's own position: that is, whether the individual voter feels that he or she would be better off with a given party in government. These models have been widely used to explain the electoral victories of the Conservative Party in the 1980s. As the Conservative Party was associated with lower taxation, people believed they would be better off (financially) under a Conservative government. These models also underpinned the Labour Party's campaign advertising during the 1997 election campaign, when much of the advertising focused on taxation and tried to reassure people that taxes would not go up under a 'New Labour' government. The sociotropic models, on the other hand, are based on evaluations of the economic position of the nation as a whole: that is, whether or not the fortunes of the national economy are best served by a particular party. Again these models have been widely used to explain Conservative victories in recent elections, and featured in their advertising during the 1997 campaign under the guise of 'Britain is booming'.

Earlier work on voting behaviour in Scotland has suggested that the Scottish National Party vote could be understood using a model of sociotropic economic voting, whereby a feeling of economic deprivation relative to the rest of Great Britain, coupled with a belief that independence for Scotland would improve this position, led to a vote for the SNP (Brand et al, 1994). Can these economic models of voting be used to explain the outcome of the referendum in Scotland?

In order to test these propositions in relation to the referendum questions, we asked our respondents to answer a series of questions on their expectations of a Scottish Parliament. These were 'Now supposing that a Scottish Parliament within the UK were set up. As a result of this Scottish Parliament, would unemployment in Scotland become higher, lower or would it make no difference?' with similarly worded questions about taxation, and (with 'better' substituted for 'higher', etc) the economy, education, the NHS and social welfare.

The results in Table 6.2 show that people in Scotland believed that the introduction of a Scottish Parliament was likely to make taxation higher, with 57 per cent expecting taxes to go up. These figures show quite clearly that the Scots were not going 'blindly' along the path to home rule as was suggested by the British Conservative leader William Hague during the campaign. Rather they were fully aware that the Parliament was likely to increase taxes in Scotland (the much publicised 'Tartan Tax') and voted in favour of the Parliament regardless. On other issues only a minority expected the position to worsen and in most cases a majority expected things to get better (the exception being on unemployment where 37 per cent expected there to be no change).

Table 6.2:   Expected effects of Scottish Parliament

	Economy	Unem- ployment	Education	NHS	Welfare	Tax
Lot better	13	6	18	16	8	0
Little Better	42	32	45	44	40	9
No change	23	37	25	25	36	25
Little worse	11	10	3	4	5	49
Lot worse	3	4	1	1	1	8
Don't Know/ Not answered	8	11	8	10	10	9
N (=100%)	852	852	852	852	852	852

Source: Scottish Election Survey 1997.

For unemployment and taxation 'better' corresponds to 'lower', etc.

Using an egocentric model of voting we would expect to find that those who thought taxation would be higher after the introduction of a Parliament were inclined to vote against the Parliament, and especially against the Parliament's having tax-varying powers. Table 6.3 looks at the intended vote in the referendum according to expectations of taxation if a Parliament were introduced.

In this table we have collapsed the categories shown in Table 6.2 into two groups, those who expected taxes to be higher (either a little or a lot) and those who expected taxation either to remain unchanged or to be lower. This allows for a clear contrast between the pessimists and optimists on this issue. As the table shows, the expectations which people held about taxation after the introduction of a Parliament are not good predictors of intended referendum vote. Whilst a higher proportion of the group that expected higher taxes intended to vote No-No, this still only represents one fifth of this group: over half still intended to vote Yes-Yes. These results seem to fly in the face of the models of rational choice discussed above. People in Scotland were not only aware of the likelihood of higher taxes but, in addition, this expectation did not lead them to vote No.

Table 6.3: **Expectations of tax rises and intended referendum vote**

	Yes-Yes	Yes-No	No-No	No-Yes	Other	N (=100%)
Taxes higher	58	9	21	5	7	477
Taxes Unchanged/ lower	65	12	8	2	13	294

Source: Scottish Election Survey 1997.

On the face of it, this evidence seems to suggest that rational-choice models of the vote do not explain the referendum result in Scotland. However, the position is altered if we look at rational voting as an exercise in cost-benefit analysis. Perhaps people are willing to pay more taxes if they perceive that the higher taxes will result in other benefits. That is, their egocentric evaluations may take second place to their sociotropic evaluations.

To test this proposition, a scale of benefits was constructed. Excluding taxation, each of the other five variables (as shown in Table 6.2) was collapsed to be either a positive response or no change/lower/worse. The scale was then simply constructed counting each of the items on which people expected a benefit. Thus, the scale runs from zero (where the respondent expected none of these items to improve) to five (where they expected all five areas to improve). The distribution of respondents on this scale is shown in Table 6.4. The table shows that, as well as the awareness of the 'Tartan Tax', people made distinctions about which areas would improve. There was not a simple divide between those expecting everything to get better and those who expected everything to get worse. Around a quarter of our respondents expected there to be no benefits of a Scottish Parliament, whilst a fifth expected everything to get better.

Table 6.4:   Number of expected benefits of Scottish Parliament

	Number of benefits expected
0	24
1	9
2	11
3	14
4	23
5	20
N (=100%)	852

Source: Scottish Election Survey 1997.

In order to answer the question posed above we need to compare the expectations people held on taxation with the benefits they expected from the Parliament. Table 6.5 does this, looking only at those who expected taxes to increase.

It is quite clear from this table that people were prepared to support a Parliament, despite expecting higher taxes, if and only if they expected the Parliament to bring wider benefits. Of those who expected higher taxes but who did not expect any wider social benefits just eight per cent intended to vote Yes-Yes in the referendum. However, amongst those who expected higher taxes and one benefit this proportion increase to 38 per cent and amongst those expecting three or more benefits from the Parliament over three quarters intended to vote Yes-Yes.

This simple analysis suggests that the expectations which people held of a Scottish Parliament were a key determinant of the referendum

Table 6.5:   Expected benefits of Scottish Parliament and
              intended referendum vote, among those who
              expected higher taxes

	Yes-Yes	Yes-No	No-No	No-Yes	Other	N (=100%)
Number of expected benefits						
0	8	10	57	12	13	110
1	38	7	34	11	10	53
2	43	13	26	4	15	53
3	78	11	6	2	2	58
4	87	7	1	1	5	114
5	87	10	0	2	1	89

Source: Scottish Election Survey 1997.

outcome. It also suggests that an expectation of a 'Tartan Tax' did not deter people from supporting the Parliament. However, these claims need to be evaluated alongside other competing models of referendum vote. Models based on social location and on national identity are looked at below. However, in a more sophisticated statistical model of these processes the findings described above were confirmed. A logistic regression model (see Appendix) was used to assess the relative impact of a number of factors on the likelihood of someone intending to vote Yes-Yes. This model showed that other factors, such as social class, gender and national identity, had only a small impact on intended vote, whilst the impact of expected benefits of the Parliament remained significant even after taking these other factors into account. In addition, there was no significant impact of expectations of tax rises after the level of expected benefits was taken into account. These models and the evidence presented above suggest that an economic model of voting based on egocentric evaluations cannot explain the referendum outcome. A rational model based an a sociotropic evaluation of benefits of the Parliament does explain the outcome. This is what we mean by 'welfare rationality': people supported a Parliament because they believed that it would improve the quality of public welfare in Scotland.

Social Location

As we mentioned earlier, in the 1950s and 1960s models of voting behaviour were based largely on the social location of voters. Put simply, it was argued that people in the working class voted Labour and those in the middle class voted Conservative (Butler and Stokes, 1969). There has been much debate in recent years about the extent to which these old alignments still explain voting behaviour in general elections (Sarlvik and Crewe, 1983; Heath et al, 1985, 1987, 1991). However, models based on social location (and social class in particular) have been used to explain voting patterns in Scotland. Here it is argued that the Conservative Party do poorly in Scotland as there are fewer of their 'natural' supporters (the middle classes) than in other parts of Great Britain (but see Brown et al (1996) for a critique of this theory). To explain the election victories of the Conservatives during the 1980s many commentators pointed to the 'extension of popular capitalism' (Heath et al, 1991), in other words to the fact that Thatcherism as a project had converted many of those who had been 'working class' into home owners and share owners – thus making them more ready to support the Conservatives. These particular social changes appeared to have less impact in Scotland (although reliable data sources are scarce). To what extent, then, can intended referendum vote be explained in terms of the social location of voters?

Table 6.6 looks at the sex, age, religion and social class of respondents to assess how, if at all, these are related to intended referendum vote. Social class is measured – as before – according to the categories developed by Goldthorpe (Heath et al, 1991).

The table does show some differences among social groups, especially in terms of social class. However, despite these differences, the largest proportion of each group intended to vote Yes-Yes. Among the small group of petty bourgeoisie we find the highest likelihood of a No-No vote, at 31 per cent. However, even in this group 42 per cent

Table 6.6: **Social characteristics and intended referendum vote**

	Yes-Yes	Yes-No	No-No	No-Yes	Other	N (=100%)
Sex						
Male	60	12	16	4	8	361
Female	57	9	15	4	16	491
Age						
18-24	67	13	12	0	7	76
25-34	69	9	9	4	10	159
35-44	62	9	13	4	13	148
45-54	56	10	24	3	8	144
55-64	58	12	12	5	13	124
over 65	44	8	22	8	18	192
Religion						
None	67	10	12	3	9	255
Catholic	60	14	13	0	13	123
Protestant	55	9	20	6	11	408
Social Class						
Salariat	48	12	25	6	9	205
Routine non-manual	65	5	16	5	9	181
Petty bourgeoisie	42	0	31	6	22	52
Manual Foremen and Supervisors	58	16	14	4	7	70
Working Class	67	11	6	2	14	286

Source: Scottish Election Survey 1997.

intended to vote Yes-Yes. Perhaps surprisingly there are few differences among the religious groups in their intended vote, with a majority of both Catholic identifiers and Protestant identifiers intending to vote Yes-Yes. There is no strong tendency for young people to be more in favour of a Parliament than older people: there is clear support on both questions in all the age groups apart from among those aged over 65.

The data in Table 6.6 suggest that a model based on social location cannot explain the referendum outcome. This is further confirmed by the statistical modelling described above, in which social class and gender were included alongside expectations of benefits and of taxes and national identity. In these models social class had only a small impact on the referendum vote, with members of the salariat and manual foremen being less likely to intend to vote Yes-Yes than members of the working class.

National Identity

National identity does not explain more than a small part of the referendum outcome either. There are good reasons to test such a model, because it is the dominant one both in political beliefs about what influences people's attitudes to the constitution, and in the academic writing on this subject. At the political level, all sides in the debate about a Scottish Parliament over the last couple of decades have made some use of national identity in an attempt to increase their vote. This has been strongest from the opponents of any Scottish Parliament and from those who favour independence. For example, when he was Prime Minister, John Major frequently spoke of the Britishness of Scotland and the history which Scotland had shared with England for three centuries (Finlay, 1997). Correspondingly, cultural nationalist have suggested that Scottish culture requires a Scottish Parliament if it is to survive (Scott, 1989). Even the supporters of home rule (as opposed to independence) have invoked Scottish identity as one argument for a Parliament: this strand can be found in, for example, the Claim of Right for Scotland which preceded the setting up of the Constitutional Convention and which, therefore, led to the proposals that were voted on in the referendum (Edwards, 1989) .

Similar views can be found among academics. Thus all the most influential writers about nationalism, despite the great differences among their interpretations, attach some importance to national identity as an explanation of why people support or oppose self government. The dispute between Gellner and Nairn on the one hand (Gellner, 1983; Nairn, 1989, 1997) and Smith (1991) on the other, significant though it is, is about how nationalist movements mobilise national identity, not about whether they do so: they disagree over the extent to which that national identity was mainly invented along with industrialism (Gellner and Nairn), or was made up of much more ancient elements (Smith). Anderson (1983), too, does not question the importance of national identity: his contribution was to explain how it could be disseminated to a mass audience (through the new print media of the nineteenth century). Many other writers have explored the ways in which the political use of national identity is not only the preserve of opposition movements. For example, Kellas talks of the 'official nationalism' of the state (Kellas, 1991): in Scotland, an instance would be the rhetoric from John Major about Britishness. Billig (1995) has pointed out that state-sponsored identity does not have to be strident to be politically effective. It can be the taken-for-granted background to everyday life.

Our data do not provide tests of all these theories in their full complexity: we are looking only at the immediate influences on people's vote on one specific set of proposals in the referendum in September 1997. Nevertheless, the data do allow us to examine the importance of national identity in explaining the positions which people take when faced with a crucial decision about the future of the overlapping nations in which they are living.

Table 6.7 shows the intended referendum vote according to the non-exclusive categories of national identity that were used in earlier chapters. The striking conclusion, in the light of all the debate, is how unimportant national identity was in explaining the vote. For each category of allegiance, a clear majority intended to vote Yes on both referendum questions. Thus, even people who expressed some allegiance to an idea of Britishness voted 65 per cent in favour of a Parliament, and 57 per cent in favour of its having tax-varying powers (these figures include responses concealed in the 'other' category in the table). Whatever weak effect Britishness may have had on the referendum vote, it certainly did not force people into opposition to the proposals. Furthermore, people who felt English apparently saw no incompatibility between that identity and supporting a Parliament for the nation in which they had come to live.

Table 6.7: **National identities and intended referendum vote**

	Yes-Yes	Yes-No	No-No	No-Yes	Other	N (=100%)
Scottish	62	10	14	4	11	678
English	54	16	16	5	9	37
British	50	12	22	5	10	448
European	63	5	16	6	10	76

Source: Scottish Election Survey 1997.

Not surprisingly, in the light of the data in Table 6.7, the measures of national identity were much less powerful explanations of referendum vote than were the expectations of the Parliament or party vote (to which we return below). Thus, in a logistic regression which analysed the intended vote on the first question in the referendum, Scottish, European and English identities had no effect at all beyond people's expectations of the Parliament and their party vote in the general election. British identity was associated with being slightly less likely to vote Yes, but was a weaker predictor than expectations of the Parliament for the economy and the health service, and was much the same strength as expectations for education and for unemployment. The pattern was similar for the second question.

The essential irrelevance of national identity to the intended referendum vote is probably a signal of the success of Labour's strategy of associating its proposals for a Scottish Parliament with renewing British democracy. Indeed, people who believed that Blair was going to be an effective prime minister were more favourable to a Parliament than people who did not, even after taking account of partisanship: thus, Labour supporters who admired Blair were more likely to intend to vote Yes than Labour supporters who were more sceptical of him. This success for Blair's approach can be seen further from Table 6.8, which shows intended referendum vote according to how the respondent felt about keeping the UK united. It is true that people who did care about this were more likely to oppose a Parliament in the referendum than those who did not care about it: thus the No votes were between 30 per cent and 40 per cent among people who agreed or strongly agreed that the UK government should keep the Union together, in contrast to about ten per cent or less among people who disagreed or strongly disagreed. Nevertheless, the resonance of Blair's strategy is seen in each of these groups. Even people who felt strongly that the UK should be kept united were evenly balanced in their attitude to a Parliament, 53 per cent voting Yes on the first question and 48 per cent doing so on the second. Voting Yes was largely not seen as a way of breaking up the Union.

Table 6.8: **Views on 'government should do everything possible to keep Britain united' and intended referendum vote**

	Yes-Yes	Yes-No	No-No	No-Yes	Other	N (=100%)
strongly agree	41	12	34	6	7	116
agree	44	12	24	7	15	317
neither agree nor disagree	60	13	7	1	19	124
disagree	84	7	4	2	3	225
strongly disagree	78	8	3	3	8	47

Source: Scottish Election Survey 1997.

When we thus conclude that national identity was only weakly relevant to the referendum outcome, we should, more correctly, say that this is about *personal* national identity (Cohen, 1996). Indeed, in one sense our findings on the expected benefits show a strong faith that Scottish social institutions can work in harmony with the new Parliament[5]. Many historians and sociologists have argued that the political aspects of Scottish national identity are mainly about institutional loyalty (McCrone, 1992; Paterson, 1994); it appears that the referendum may have represented a culmination of that. Rational welfare choices always take place in the context of a specific set of national institutions, in Scotland as much as elsewhere. In this sense, rational calculation, far from precluding national allegiance, actually depends on it. But that allegiance can come from people of diverse personal identities.

THE SCOTTISH PARLIAMENT AND THE GENERAL ELECTION

The Conservative Party believed that their stance on the constitution in the 1992 general election had won them votes in Scotland, and that, in particular, it was the tactic which saved them from the collapse which both they and most observers expected (Lang, 1994b). In the 1997 general election, they therefore tried the same tactic again. Indeed, in the final few days of the campaign, the prime minister John Major toured Wales, Northern Ireland and Scotland reiterating his belief that the Union was beneficial to all its partners, and that it was threatened by Labour's proposals for a Scottish Parliament and a Welsh Assembly.

Scottish Labour, on the other hand, had come to believe firmly and almost unanimously in its policy on home rule. That policy may have started expediently in the 1970s as a response to the rise of the SNP, but, by the time of John Smith's leadership between 1992 and 1994, it had become a matter of principle (Brown et al 1996, Chapter Six). The main reason for the change was the party's work with the Liberal Democrats and various civic bodies in the Constitutional Convention between 1989 and 1995. The consensus which Labour could thus feel they were leading lasted through the referendum campaign itself, and, indeed, broadened significantly to include the SNP.

---

[5] We are grateful to Neil MacCormick for the point in this paragraph.

Labour also, however, feared that the Conservatives may have been correct that they had gained from their opposition to home rule in 1992. They also feared that the proposal to give a Scottish Parliament powers to vary income tax would be used by the Conservatives throughout Britain to claim that Labour really believed in increasing taxes after all, despite protestations to the contrary by the Shadow Chancellor, Gordon Brown. That is one reason why, in the summer of 1996, they announced their intention to hold a referendum on their proposals, with a separate question on the proposed taxation powers (Jones, 1997). They hoped that this would deflect Conservative criticism during the general election campaign: Labour would be able to say that decisions about home rule and about tax would be taken by people in Scotland themselves in a separate vote.

To many commentators, this move by Labour appeared to have worked. The constitutional issue seemed to play a less prominent role in the 1997 general election than it had done in 1992, despite Major's attempts to repeat his themes. The Conservative collapse in the 1997 election was taken by some opponents of home rule as confirmation of that: they claimed that voters felt safe about voting against the Conservatives because they knew that this would not automatically translate into a threat to the Union.

And yet the referendum delivered an emphatic endorsement of Labour's policy, and – as we have seen – this happened despite a widespread belief that taxes would rise. So was the constitution an issue in the election? Did it contribute to the Conservatives' losses? Did the Conservatives get their message about the effects of a Parliament across?

The first point to note is that 50 per cent of people in the survey said that the issue of a Scottish Parliament was important to them in deciding how they would vote in the general election. That does not suggest that the matter had been wholly removed from the election in the way that Labour had intended. But Table 6.9 shows that the effects of the issue were not as favourable to the Conservatives as they hoped and as Labour and the Liberal Democrats feared. For each party, this table displays the referendum intentions among three groups of people: for example, those who recalled voting Conservative in 1992, those who still identified with the Conservative Party in 1997, and those

Table 6.9: **Attachment to parties and intended referendum vote**

	Yes-Yes	Yes-No	No-No	No-Yes	Other	N (=100%)
Conservative						
recalls voting Conservative in 1992	30	10	42	7	11	157
identifies with Conservatives	25	11	47	7	10	140
voted Conservative in 1997	15	8	59	10	9	100
Labour						
recalls voting Labour in 1992	67	12	7	3	11	316
identifies with Labour	63	12	8	2	14	397
voted Labour in 1997	64	12	9	2	12	353
Liberal Democrat						
recalls voting Liberal Democrat in 1992	57	5	20	7	12	63
identifies with Liberal Democrats	56	9	15	10	11	90
voted Liberal Democrat in 1997	57	10	16	6	11	87

[Table 6.9 continued on next page]

[Table 6.9 continued]

	Yes-Yes	Yes-No	No-No	No-Yes	Other	N (=100%)
SNP						
recalls voting SNP in 1992	82	6	4	3	5	105
identifies with SNP	87	6	1	2	11	140
voted SNP in 1997	78	7	4	4	7	129

Source: Scottish Election Survey 1997.

who actually voted Conservative in 1997. (Identifiers were those who chose the Conservatives in response to the question 'generally speaking, do you think of yourself as ... '.) These can be taken as three increasingly strong measures of attachment to the party. For this purpose, it does not matter whether people were accurate in their recall of their 1992 vote: their response to that is merely a measure of some willingness to acknowledge a past association with the party. The main message of the table is that the Conservatives lost the votes of many of those among their supporters who intended to vote in favour of a Parliament. Thus, whereas 42 per cent of people who recalled voting Conservative in 1992 intended to vote Yes on the first question, that proportion was only 38 per cent of those who still identified with the Conservatives, and a mere 24 per cent of 1997 Conservative voters (these figures again include a few responses from the 'other' category). So a first inference from the table is that the Conservatives' stance on the constitution lost them votes. It was one reason why – as we saw in Chapter Three (Table 3.4) – the Conservatives were driven back onto a small core of people who voted habitually for the party.

This interpretation is confirmed by four further pieces of statistical analysis. The first is that, for the other three main parties, the referendum intentions were similar among their voters, their identifiers and their previous voters (Table 6.9). For example, whereas the 'Yes-

Yes' proportion among 1997 Conservative voters was only 50 per cent of the proportion among 1992 Conservative voters (15 per cent as a proportion of 30 per cent), the 1997 Labour proportion was 96 per cent of the 1992 Labour proportion (64 per cent as a proportion of 67 per cent). For Liberal Democrats, these proportions did not differ at all (both 57 per cent), and for the SNP the 1997 proportion was 95 per cent of the 1992 proportion (78 per cent compared with 82 per cent). So most people had already accepted these parties' stances long before the general election, and were not either attracted or deterred any further.

Second, people who identified in some way with the Conservatives in 1997 and who supported a Scottish Parliament were more likely to say that the issue of a Parliament was an important influence on their vote than people who identified with the Conservatives and who opposed a Parliament. For example, among people who recalled voting Conservative in 1992 and who intended to vote Yes on the first question in the referendum, 43 per cent said that the issue was important; among those 1992 Conservatives who intended to vote No, only 34 per cent said it was important. Previous Conservatives who supported a Parliament and who believed that the issue was important were faced with only two options in the general election: abandon their party or abandon the Parliament. The fall-off in Conservative support among such people suggests that they tended to choose to abandon the party.

Third, the fall-off in Conservative vote seen here was not found in 1992, the election when the Conservatives believed that this issue bolstered their vote. In the absence of specific referendum proposals in 1992, there is no direct comparison to Table 6.9, but we can look instead at general attitudes to a Scottish Parliament. The election surveys in both 1992 and 1997 asked what is now a standard question about options for governing Scotland. In the 1992 election study, 72 per cent of the whole sample opted for either home rule or independence; in 1997, the proportion was much the same, at 77 per cent. In 1997, as in the specific questions on the referendum, support for some kind of Parliament was higher among Conservative identifiers (47 per cent) than among Conservative voters (38 per cent), and for the other parties there was no difference (as in Table 6.9). But in 1992 there was almost no such difference for the Conservatives either (44 per cent for identifiers and 41 per cent for voters). These figures suggest that the Conservatives' stance in 1997 was off-putting in a way that it had not been five years earlier.

The fourth reason to believe that the Conservatives lost support as a result of their opposition to a Scottish Parliament comes from a more rigorous analysis of the data in Table 6.9. One objection to the interpretation that we have made is that the loss of Conservative support could, perhaps, be explained by factors other than the constitutional issue. For example, it is generally agreed that the Conservatives lost votes throughout Britain because they were no longer seen as capable of being a strong government and because some of their MPs had been the subject of political scandal (for example, allegedly taking bribes for asking Parliamentary questions). If Conservative identifiers who believed these accusations were also more likely than other Conservatives to believe in a Scottish Parliament, then the patterns in Table 6.9 could be explained by these attitudes to leadership capacity and to politicians' honesty rather than by attitudes to home rule.

The way to test this is to control for various other factors which predict the Conservative vote well, and then to see whether referendum intention continues to be associated with Conservative vote. Consider, for example, all those people who still believed that the Conservatives were capable of running a strong government. Of those in this group who recalled voting Conservative in 1992, 29 per cent intended to vote Yes on the first referendum question; of those who voted Conservative in 1997, 26 per cent intended to do so. Thus, even among those who continued to admire the Conservatives' capacity for firm leadership, intentions for the referendum seemed to influence their decision as to whether to remain with the Conservatives in 1997.

The more thorough way of doing this using many predictors of Conservative vote is, again, logistic regression. Account was taken of 31 factors which predict Conservative vote – attitudes to the record of the Conservative government on keeping their promises, standing up for Britain, and exercising strong government; attitudes to their record on crime, education, the health service, prices, standard of living, tax and unemployment; attitudes to John Major; beliefs as to whether

Conservative MPs were more open to bribery than other MPs; general views about policies on poverty, private medicine, spending on the health service, education and defence; beliefs about whether workers should have more say in the running of industry and whether there should be redistribution of wealth; attitudes to Britain's membership of the European Union; attitudes to the effectiveness of British state institutions and to British cultural values (see Chapter Four and Heath and Taylor (1996); Heath and Kellas (1998)); general views on the moral standards of British public life; and general demographic variables (age, sex and social class). So this was a very strong set of controls. It was able accurately to predict 94 per cent of the decisions of the whole sample to vote or not vote for the Conservatives in 1997 (including 69 per cent of the decisions to vote Conservative); 82 per cent of those decisions among 1992 Conservative (including 84 per cent of the decisions to vote Conservative); and 84 per cent of those decisions among Conservative identifiers (including 91 per cent of the decisions to vote Conservative). And yet, for each of these predictions, intentions for the first referendum question remained as a further predictor of 1997 Conservative vote. For the analysis involving the whole sample (comparing Conservative voters with all other electors), referendum intention was a stronger predictor of Conservative vote than all others except views on the Conservatives' record in dealing with unemployment (with which it was equally strong). For the analysis involving only 1992 Conservative voters, referendum intention was as strong a predictor of Conservative vote as age and as a tendency to blame the Conservatives for a drop in the average standard of living, and was stronger than all other predictors. Among Conservative identifiers, referendum intention was a stronger predictor of Conservative vote than any other variable. In none of these analyses was the intention for the second referendum question influential on the Conservative vote over and above the effect of the intention on the first question.

So here we have a stringent test of the claim that the Conservatives lost votes because of their stance on the constitution. Even when we take account of all the other reasons why the Conservatives lost votes, we still find evidence that people were influenced in their attitude to the Conservatives by the party's attitudes to a Scottish Parliament.

One of the reasons the Conservatives lost votes in this way was the point we have already noted about Britishness and attitudes to home rule. Blair and the Labour Party seem to have persuaded people that being British was consistent with supporting a Parliament. The implications of this for the Conservatives can be seen further if we look at the small group of people who rate their Britishness higher than their Scottishness. This came in response to the question we described in Chapter Three which asked people to place themselves on a scale ranging from 'Scottish, not British' at one end to 'British, not Scottish' at the other. Just eight per cent of the sample chose to rate their Britishness ahead of their Scottishness, a similar proportion to the five per cent who did so in 1992. But, in 1992, this group had been very clearly sympathetic to the Conservatives, as Table 6.10 shows. They had also been at best sceptical about home rule (as evidenced by the general question about constitutional change). By 1997, the Conservative vote among them had collapsed to just 19 per cent, and the support for home rule had risen to 61 per cent. The continuing low level of support for independence among these people tends to confirm that we are seeing here evidence of a redefinition of Britishness rather than a threat to it. Asserting Britishness acquired a new political meaning between 1992 and 1997, no longer closely tied to voting Conservative or to being wary of a Scottish Parliament.

Moreover, if the Conservatives lost the argument over the alleged threat which a Parliament would pose to Britishness, they also lost the votes of people who did not believe their detailed case on the effects of a Parliament. Table 6.11 shows the number of benefits which people expected from the Parliament, separately for 1992 Conservatives, for Conservative identifiers, and for 1997 Conservatives. The Conservative arguments on this seemed to have had only a weak effect, even with their core support. Around one half of Conservative identifiers and previous supporters expected some benefits from the Parliament, and just under one half of 1997 Conservative voters expected some benefits. Thus, when the British Conservative leader William Hague reacted on 12 September 1997 to the referendum result by claiming it was a 'sad day for Scotland', he was apparently not in tune with the people whom the Conservatives must win back if they are to recover their electoral position in Scotland.

Table 6.10: Conservative vote and constitutional preference, 1992 and 1997, among those who identified themselves as 'British more than Scottish' or 'British not Scottish'

	1992 (%)	1997 (%)
voted Conservative	53	19
home rule	43	61
independence	7	10
N (=100%)	58	66

Source: Scottish Election Surveys 1992 and 1997.

Table 6.11: Attachment to Conservative Party and expectations of benefits from Scottish Parliament

	number of benefits expected						
	0	1	2	3	4	5	N (=100%)
recalls voting Conservative in 1992	44	19	12	10	10	6	157
identifies with Conservatives	51	20	11	7	8	3	140
voted Conservative in 1997	58	23	9	7	3	1	100

Source: Scottish Election Survey 1997.

CONCLUSION

We have argued three main points in this chapter. The first is that intentions for the referendum were shaped by the expectations which people had of what a Parliament would do. The result in the referendum was decisive because most people expected clear welfare benefits, and because they expected higher taxes to be used to pay for these. This happened despite the fact that – as we saw in Chapter Five – Scotland does not differ from the rest of Britain in attitudes in most of the policy areas that will be transferred to the Parliament. The referendum showed that Scots had found a distinctive route to policy destinations that were mostly shared widely.

The second point is that intentions for the referendum were not shaped by social structure or by identity, but by issues of welfare. The referendum vote was fairly uniform across all social classes, all age groups, and both sexes. It was not strongly influenced by personal national identity, probably because the Labour Party and Tony Blair had successfully appealed to a sense of modernising Britishness as one reason for supporting change. Feeling Scottish was certainly one influence on voting in favour, but feeling British was not mainly a reason to vote against. At the same time, despite the only weak relevance of personal national identity, the referendum result probably did owe a great deal to a widespread faith that Scottish institutions would work with a Parliament to deliver better social welfare.

The third point is that the Conservative Party lost votes in the general election because of its stance on the constitution. They lost the argument both with the electorate as a whole, and with people who generally thought of themselves as Conservative supporters. If they are to recover in Scotland, then they will have to find a way of working constructively with and in the new Parliament, in order to exorcise the memories of their intransigence through their electoral debacle of the 1997 general election.

7

The Future of Scottish Politics

INTRODUCTION

Speculation about the future of Scottish politics is easy; prediction is much more difficult. This final chapter attempts to predict on the basis of the speculations of the respondents to two surveys: the Scottish Election Survey and the Scottish Referendum Survey, both of 1997. These speculations are much more relevant to the future of Scottish politics now than they might have been in the past, because the new Scottish Parliament will allow popular views about the future to influence that future as never before. Nevertheless, even in a democracy the future is not determined by speculation, however representative; in particular, the imagination which people bring to bear on politics will itself change in response to the coming of the Parliament, whereas the views we summarise here have largely been formed by the existing constitutional structures and ways of making policy.

The chapter analyses three aspects of the future. The first relates to expectations of the Scottish Parliament. We saw in Chapter Six that expectations on policy were the strongest predictors of vote in the referendum. But what about expectations of the Parliament as a new democratic body – its responsiveness to Scots, or its capacity to represent Scotland to the wider world? How do these expectations about democratic effectiveness relate to expectations about policy? Are democratic expectations any more strongly related to a sense of national identity than was the referendum vote (Chapter Six)? And will democratic expectations be a stronger influence on how people vote in elections to the Scottish Parliament than expectations about policy or attitudes to the political parties? In short, this first dimension of analysis concerns the ways in the which the new Parliament might operate.

The second dimension is how it might evolve. Once it is set up, the main constitutional question in Scottish politics will be whether the country will move towards full independence. How likely do people expect that to be? Is any evolution in that direction feared or desired? Are the people who expect a move to independence those who have low expectations of the Parliament in relation to policy or to democratic effectiveness? Does expecting independence express an aspect of Scottish identity? On the other hand, what residual support is likely to remain for the current constitutional position – that is, for no elected body at all or for a weaker one than will be set up in 1999?

How this develops will depend as much on the standing of the Scottish political parties as directly on popular views. Is there evidence that the Conservatives could begin to recover their position in the Parliamentary elections? If so, from which other parties would they be likely to gain extra votes? Is the SNP likely to perform better in Scottish elections than in those to Westminster? This is the position in Catalonia, after all, where the main nationalist party does much better in elections to the Catalan Parliament than in state-wide elections to the Cortes in Madrid; as we saw in Chapter One, several opinion polls in spring 1998 suggested that the SNP would indeed gain in this way. In understanding the voting patterns for the Parliament, to what should we pay most attention? We can test this question for expectations about policy, about democratic effectiveness and about the likely evolution of the Parliament, and for the more diffuse concept of trusting the various parties to represent Scottish interests. So this analysis tells us which party will be best able to inherit the high expectations which people have of the new Parliament.

DEMOCRATIC EFFECTIVENESS

Three questions in the Scottish Referendum Survey relate to the democratic effectiveness of the new Parliament. These asked about whether the Parliament would give people a greater say in how Scotland is governed, and about whether it would give Scotland a stronger voice in the UK and the European Union. The responses are shown in Table 7.1. As with the expectations of policy that we looked at in Chapter Six, the clear impression here is of optimism. Nearly four out of five people expect the Parliament to be responsive to people in Scotland, 70 per cent expect it to give Scotland a stronger voice in the UK, and 60 per cent expect it to do the same for the EU (even though the Parliament will have no statutory powers in relation to the EU). These optimistic expectations tend to cluster together. For example, 78 per cent of people who expect the Parliament to give Scots more say in government also expect it to give Scotland a stronger voice in the UK, and 68 per cent of them expect this also in the EU. Likewise, 73 per cent of those who expect Scotland's voice in the UK to be strengthened expect the same in the EU.

Not surprisingly, moreover, the optimism is greatest among those who voted in favour of the Parliament in the referendum. For example, whereas 92 per cent of those who voted Yes-Yes expect the Parliament to be responsive to Scots, only 43 per cent of those who voted No-No expect that (still, though, a substantial group). Similarly, among Yes-Yes voters, the proportion expecting a stronger voice for Scotland was 85 per cent for the UK and 80 per cent for the EU; the corresponding proportions for No-No voters were 24 per cent and just 13 per cent.

So the new institution starts out with a deep reservoir of optimism about its capacity to enhance the quality of democracy in Scotland. As it evolves, however, the question will be how these expectations relate to other influences on political attitudes. Are these expectations of democratic effectiveness strong enough to push the Parliament towards taking them seriously?

The first way to test this is to assess whether the democratic expectations are truly national. Is the optimism shared among various social groups, in the same way as the Yes votes were in the referendum (see Chapter Six)? To assess this, the variables recording democratic expectations were modelled by logistic regression (in each

Table　7.1:　　**Expected　democratic　effectiveness　of　the Scottish　Parliament**

	More say	Stronger voice in UK	Stronger voice in EU
Yes	79	70	60
No	2	9	11
No difference	19	20	29
N (=100%)	676	676	676

Source: Scottish Referendum Survey 1997.

Full wording of the questions:

1. 'Would a Scottish Parliament give ordinary Scottish people more say in how Scotland is governed/less say/make no difference?'.

2. 'Would a Scottish Parliament give Scotland a stronger voice in the United Kingdom/a weaker voice in the United Kingdom/make no difference?'.

3. 'Would a Scottish Parliament give Scotland a stronger voice in the European Union/a weaker voice in the European Union/make no difference?'.

case contrasting the 'Yes' category in Table 7.1 with the other two); the explanatory variables were social class, sex, age, housing tenure and education level. The striking general result is how few of these variables have any effect on the measures of democratic effectiveness. There were no differences at all in relation to social class, sex, or tenure. For being responsive to Scots, the only effect was in relation to education level, where people with less education had higher expectations than people with more. But the differences were not great: for example, while 81 per cent of people who left school at ages 16 or younger expected more responsiveness, the proportion for people who stayed in full-time education until ages over 19 was still a substantial 72 per cent. For giving Scotland a greater say in the UK, again education level was the only variable which had an effect, but again every group had a majority of optimists: 74 per cent for people who had left school by age 16, and 56 per cent for people who stayed on into post-school education. For Scotland's voice in the EU, the only variable which had an effect was age, but – once more – the variation was slight: for example, 64 per cent of people aged under 45 were optimists, and 57 per cent of people aged 45 or older.

In short, there is evidence that the optimism is truly national. This is firm social ground on which to build a new democracy, based as that is on assumptions about equal citizenship, not structured by class, sex, age and so on (Hall and Held, 1989). (There were too few people from minority ethnic groups in the survey to allow a separate analysis to be carried out for them.)

Next, though, on what grounds will the Parliament be judged as to its democratic effectiveness? One way of looking at this is to examine the relationship between the expectations about democracy and the expectations for policy. If the democratic expectations are closely linked to the policy variables, then it is likely that the Parliament's democratic success will be judged by whether it has delivered better public services and so on, either because democratic effectiveness is largely equated with policy effectiveness, or – more subtly – because policy outcomes will be used by the electorate as indicators of how democratic the Parliament has been. If, on the other hand, expectations about democracy seem to be somewhat independent of policy expectations, then that would be indirect evidence that people are interested in the processes of policy making and not just in the outcomes.

This issue was tested by modelling the democratic expectations in terms of the policy expectations (as defined in Table 6.2 in Chapter Six). The conclusion is strikingly different for the different dimensions of democratic effectiveness. For responsiveness to Scots, there was an association with several policy expectations – on unemployment, taxes, the economy, and social welfare. There was no association with policy expectations for health or education. For Scotland's voice in the UK, there was association only with two of these – the economy and social welfare. And for Scotland's voice in Europe, there was association with only one, the economy. These results suggest that the Parliament's democratic effectiveness will be judged by its policy effectiveness so far as its responsiveness to Scots is concerned, but will be judged by different criteria for speaking to the outside world.

Nevertheless, despite these different conclusions, there is also an important similarity which will cause the Parliament some difficulties. Those policy expectations that do relate to democratic expectations are mainly for policy areas which are not within the Parliament's powers. Thus, according to this analysis, no matter what the Parliament does for health or education, it is unlikely to persuade people that it is being democratically responsive. To achieve that, it will have to improve the economy, and yet the main relevant powers are reserved to Westminster. The same is true to some extent for social welfare, where the Parliament's capacity to have an impact will be constrained by its lack of any responsibility for social security. It is probably relevant that – as we saw in Chapter Five – these economic and welfare topics are areas where Scots are more left-wing than people in England: distinctive views, and high expectations, could push the Parliament towards seeking greater powers. We return to this point in the next section when we discuss whether the Parliament is likely to take Scotland towards independence.

An alternative way of judging the democratic effectiveness of a new national Parliament is whether it expresses the nation's sense of identity: as noted in Chapter Six, many writers on this topic assume that asserting identity is a primary reason why people support national Parliaments, and that a Parliament can, in turn, strengthen that identity. This can be tested here by analysing the association between democratic expectations and a sense of national identity. The measure of identity used is the 'Moreno' question which was discussed in Chapter Three. There was some association between identity and democratic expectations: see Table 7.2. Thus, whereas 85 per cent of people who rated their Scottishness higher than any Britishness believed that the Parliament would be responsive to Scots, the proportion was 63 per cent among the small group of people who rated their Britishness higher than any Scottishness. For strengthening Scotland's voice in the UK, the corresponding proportions were 79 per cent and 49 per cent; and for Scotland's voice in the EU, they were 67 per cent and 38 per cent. But a sense of Scottishness is simply too widespread in Scotland for these differences to matter: as the table shows, even among people who rated their Scottishness and Britishness equally, there was an optimistic majority on each measure of democratic effectiveness.

Table 7.2: **Expected democratic effectiveness of the Scottish Parliament by national identity**

	More say	Stronger voice in UK	Stronger voice in EU	N (=100%)
Scottish, not British	86	77	65	213
Scottish more than British	84	82	70	216
Equally Scottish and British	70	54	50	190
British more than Scottish	68	50	50	23
British, not Scottish	57	48	25	21

Source: Scottish Referendum Survey 1997.

The table shows percentage replying Yes (as defined in Table 7.1).

Full wording of the questions is shown in footnote to Table 7.1.

In any case, this measure of national identity turned out to be less strongly associated with democratic expectations than were the policy expectations. When the identity variable was added to the logistic regressions, it had no effect on the model for responsiveness to Scots: the influential variables continued to be expectations for unemployment, taxes, the economy, and social welfare. That is, once these were controlled for, there was no residual effect of identity at all. In other words, the pattern shown in Table 7.2 can be explained by the fact that people who tend to the Scottish end of the scale tend also to expect the Parliament to deal with unemployment etc. For giving Scotland a stronger voice in the UK, there was a weak effect of national identity over and above the effect of expectations in relation to the economy and social welfare, but the identity variable did not remove these effects. And for giving Scotland a voice in the EU, the national identity variable again had no effect at all.

So the most that can be said for national identity in these models of expectations about democratic effectiveness is that it has a weak effect. This is evidence, therefore, that the democratic credentials of the Parliament will not be judged primarily by its capacity to articulate a sense of Scottishness. In summary of the whole analysis, we can say that, while there are strong expectations that the Parliament will enhance the quality of Scottish democracy, its democratic responsiveness will be judged primarily by the policies it pursues. The problem for it is that the most relevant expectations for policy are in topics which are partly or wholly reserved to Westminster. So the next question about the future which we must address is the likelihood of the Parliament's eventually acquiring those extra powers, perhaps resulting in full independence.

INDEPENDENCE

The Scottish Referendum Survey asked people whether they thought that Scotland would leave the UK 'at any time in the next twenty years'. The results are in Table 7.3, where it can be seen that a clear majority (60 per cent) expect that to happen. At first sight, this might seem to be contrary to what people actually want: as Table 7.4 shows, at the time of the referendum, only 39 per cent favoured independence. However, this figure is substantially larger than those found in polls over the last few years (McCrone, 1997), and suggests that the sheer fact of having a Parliament might change opinion. Moreover, if we look further at people's second choice of constitutional future, a rather different picture emerges. A majority (58 per cent) of the sample gave some form of independence (in or out of the EU) as either their first or their second choice. Of those who were, in this way, reasonably open to the idea of independence, 69 per cent expected it to come about within the next two decades; of those who did not even have independence as their second choice, only 49 per cent expected it to happen. Put differently, of the people who expect independence to come about, 66 per cent are at least not opposed to that outcome.

Table 7.3:   Expectations of independence

At any time in the next twenty years, do you think it is likely or unlikely that Scotland will become completely independent from the United Kingdom?

Very likely	19
Quite likely	41
Quite unlikely	25
Very unlikely	16
N (=100%)	638

Source: Scottish Referendum Survey 1997.

Excludes 38 people who had no opinion.

Table 7.4:   Preferred constitutional status for Scotland

Scotland should become independent, separate from the UK and the European Union	9
Scotland should become independent, separate from the UK but part of the European Union	30
Scotland should remain part of the UK, with its own elected Parliament which has some taxation powers	34
Scotland should remain part of the UK, with its own elected Parliament which has no taxation powers	10
Scotland should remain part of the UK without an elected Parliament	18
N (=100%)	647

Source: Scottish Referendum Survey 1997.

Excludes 29 people who had no opinion.

So the starting point for this analysis is that a majority of people expect Scotland to become independent, and that most people do not regard that prospect with alarm. These facts on their own would tend to imply that, once the Parliament is established, the main constitutional question facing Scotland will be whether it should acquire greater powers. This is confirmed by analysing further the relationship between first and second preferences for Scotland's constitutional status. What do people do now whose preferred constitutional option was defeated in the referendum? That is, what do people do now who favoured either no elected body at all, or else one with no tax-varying powers? In fact, 29 per cent of these people gave a tax-varying Parliament as their second choice, and nine per cent gave independence as their second choice, and so nearly four of ten members of this group are probably not unhappy with the outcome. Only 17 per cent of the whole sample had both their first and their second choices baulked by the result of the referendum, hardly a large enough group to form the core of intransigent scepticism about the Parliament. Again, therefore, we are led to the conclusion that, once the Parliament is set up, the main constitutional debate will be about independence, and that reversion to the status quo ante will simply not be raised seriously.

To understand how this debate about independence might develop, we can look at some explanations of why a majority believes that independence will come about. There is the same range of potential explanations as was used in Chapter Six to analyse the referendum result – in terms of social structure, policy expectations of the Parliament, and national identity. Following our analysis earlier in this chapter, we can also add democratic expectations of the Parliament. The statistical model used was a logistic regression, contrasting the belief that independence was 'very likely' or 'quite likely' with all other categories of response.

For social structure, the story is also the usual one of almost no effect. Social class, sex, age and education had no influence on whether people expect independence. There was a weak association with housing tenure, but mainly because people in the small private rented sector were less likely to expect independence than people in the other types of tenure.

There are potentially contradictory reasons to believe that the policy expectations for the Parliament would be associated with expecting Scotland to become independent. On the one hand, it could be the case that people who expect the Parliament to be unable to deliver effective policies would be most likely to expect it to acquire extra powers. This might be especially the case in policy areas for which the Parliament will not have responsibility under the Scotland Act of 1998 (in several of which – as we have seen – Scots are more left-wing than people in England). On the other hand, we might argue that people who are optimistic about the effectiveness of a Parliament with limited powers would be more likely to be confident enough to see independence as an eventual outcome.

Simple descriptions of the relationship between expecting independence and expectations for policy are shown in Table 7.5. There are two patterns. On the one hand, for education, health and social welfare, the results would straightforwardly support the second of the two arguments: the more optimistic people were about the Parliament and these policy areas, generally the more likely they were to expect independence. On the other hand, for the state of the Scottish economy, for unemployment and for tax, the results seem to support both arguments at the same time. The strongest expectations of independence were at each end of the response distribution. Thus 66 per cent of people who expected the economy to get a lot or a little better expected independence to come about, but so also did 53 per cent of those who expected it to get a lot or a little worse. The proportion was 42 per cent among people who expected no difference in the economy.

In the logistic regression (using the full set of categories for the expectations), only expectations for health and the state of the economy had independent effects, still following the patterns shown in the table.

So there is some evidence here that those who want the Parliament to move towards independence cannot lose. If the Parliament makes a success of the health service and of other policy areas for which it will have responsibility right from the start, then the popular expectation will be that it should take on more powers. If it fails to regenerate the economy, then it can tap into a popular mood which says that this is because it does not have enough powers to satisfy Scottish left-of-centre preferences.

Table 7.5: **Expectations of Scottish independence by expected effects of Scottish Parliament on policy**

	Economy	Unem-ployment	Taxation	Education	NHS	Welfare
better	66	62	66	65	64	63
	(406)	(277)	(25)	(456)	(421)	(370)
neither	42	51	57	44	50	53
	(171)	(257)	(144)	(176)	(196)	(249)
worse	53	66	59	44	38	50
	(78)	(117)	(485)	(21)	(37)	(34)

Source: Scottish Referendum Survey 1997.

The table shows percentage replying that independence was 'very likely' or 'quite likely' (see Table 7.3).

Sample sizes in brackets.

The response categories (rows) have been condensed from those shown in Table 6.2 (Chapter Six).

For unemployment and taxation 'better' corresponds to 'lower', etc.

Moreover, what will count here will be policy not democratic renewal. When the expectations about democratic effectiveness were added to the model, they had no influence on expecting independence over and above the variables relating to policy. This is not surprising when we consider the analysis in the last section. We found there that people would probably be inclined to judge democratic effectiveness by the effectiveness of the Parliament in policy. So when claims are made in political debate over the next few years that the Parliament has to be fully independent in order to respond to the needs of the people, the rhetoric will be about policy not directly about more abstract ideas of giving people a greater say in government or a stronger voice in the UK and the EU.

Nevertheless, a move towards independence will not only be about whether the Parliament has the capacity to deliver effective policies. It will also be about identity. People who felt most Scottish were most likely to predict that independence would come about – 74 per cent of those feeling 'Scottish, not British', but only 46 per cent of those feeling 'equally Scottish and British'. This effect of identity operated over and above the effect of the policy expectations – that is, in the logistic regression model, over and above expectations for the health service and for the economy. So, although we found in Chapter Six that national identity was not a strong predictor of vote in the referendum, we have evidence here that it might be more closely related to any evolution towards independence. That is, perhaps, not surprising, if we were correct in our analysis in Chapter Six that the relative unimportance of identity in the referendum vote reflected the success of the Labour Party in linking their proposals to a renewal of British democracy. Such an argument obviously could not work for any campaign for ending the political aspects of Britishness altogether.

POLITICAL PARTIES

Whether or not the Parliament is judged to be a democratic success or acquires greater powers will depend, however, not on abstract arguments but on the clash of political parties. Indeed, our finding that policy preferences matter above all else tends to confirm this: vague talk about renewing democracy has not resonated with people so much as quite traditional concerns with social and economic policy. So how the party battle develops will continue to be the main political question.

The first point to analyse is where the likely flows between parties might be. One way of doing that is to look at people's second preferences among the parties. These were shown in Table 3.3 (Chapter Three). There were two groupings there. Labour and the SNP are clearly interchangeable for many voters: amongst the supporters of each of these parties, the other is by far the most popular second preference. And the same goes for the Conservatives and the Liberal Democrats. So, on the basis of how people report their attitudes to the parties, we might expect flows of votes within these pairs. Since Labour polled well in May 1997, and the Conservatives exceptionally badly, the most likely drift of votes is therefore towards the SNP from Labour, and towards the Conservatives from the Liberal Democrats. The problem for the Conservatives is that there are not many votes to gain from that source (because the Liberal Democrats polled only 13 per cent of the vote).

A second way to analyse likely flows of votes is to compare the policy preferences of people who are close to each of the parties: see Table 7.6. This analysis can tell us whether the parties are competing for similar or distinct pools of voters. 'Close to' is defined here either to be a voter for the party or to give that party as a second preference. We use the Scottish Election Survey (as in Table 3.3). According to this definition, 17 per cent of the sample were close to the Conservatives, 60 per cent to Labour, 31 per cent to the Liberal Democrats, and 43 per cent to the SNP. In one sense, these figures are the current ceiling on the parties' votes (but note that they represent proportions of the whole electorate, not necessarily of people who would be likely to turn out to vote).

The table shows the policy preferences for people close to each of the parties (the same set of policy preferences as was used in Table 5.1 in Chapter Five). The most obvious first impression is that people close to the Conservatives are quite distinct on almost all the measures. The gap is particularly large (greater than ten per cent) in relation to private medicine, education, using prisons to reform criminals, redistribution of wealth, government spending to eradicate poverty, raising taxes to pay for pensions or for higher government spending, stronger laws to regulate trade unions, giving workers more say in industry, signing the EU Social Chapter, introducing a minimum wage, nationalisation and defence cuts. The second main point is how close Labour and the SNP are to each other – in every case, no more than a few percentage points apart. This shows in more detail something which we noted in Chapter Five. And, third, the Liberal Democrats generally lie between the Conservatives on the one hand and Labour and the SNP on the other, but nearly always further from the Conservatives than from the latter: only in relation to stiff sentences for criminals and to giving workers more say in industry do

Table 7.6: **Policy preferences by pools[*] of party support**

	Con	Lab	Lib Dem	SNP
Government should put more money into the NHS[1]	88	98	97	97
Government should encourage the growth of private medicine[1]	39	24	27	24
Government should spend more money on education[1]	91	97	94	96
Government should get rid of private education in Britain[1]	12	34	25	33
The cleverest children should be selected for education in separate schools[2]	46	22	32	24
It is a good thing for schools to be made to compete against each other for pupils[2]	50	19	27	20
People who break the law should be given stiffer sentences[2]	75	85	76	87
Life sentences should mean life[2]	82	88	85	90
Prisons should try harder to reform prisoners rather than just punishing them[2]	61	81	82	77
People should be allowed to use their cars as much as they like, even if it causes damage to the environment[2]	33	23	25	27
For the sake of the environment, car users should pay higher taxes[2]	20	27	30	22
Income and wealth should be redistributed towards ordinary working people[2]	39	78	63	79
Government should spend more money to get rid of poverty[1]	84	98	94	97

[Table 7.6 continued on next page]

[Table 7.6 continued]

	Con	Lab	Lib Dem	SNP
It would be better if everyone paid less tax and had to pay more towards their own health care, schools and the like[2]	21	14	15	12
Taxes should be as low as possible, and people should have to provide more for themselves even if it means that some people suffer[2]	13	6	5	6
Everyone's taxes should go up to provide better old age pensions for all[2]	45	58	60	62
Government should increase taxes and spend more on health, education and social benefits[3]	48	77	79	77
Government should introduce stricter laws to regulate the activities of trade unions[1]	42	30	30	30
Government should give workers more say in running the places where they work[1]	61	79	67	83
The British government should sign up to the Social Chapter so that British workers have the same rights at work as everyone else in Europe[4]	15	50	45	49
The law should set a minimum wage so that no employer can pay their workers too little[5]	48	83	76	82
There should be more nationalisation of companies by government[6]	7	42	33	39
Government should spend less on defence[1]	38	69	62	69
Government should give more aid to poor countries in Africa and Asia[2]	31	39	46	30
N (= 100%)	146	494	253	359

[Notes for Table 7.6 on the next page]

Notes for Table 7.6:

Source: Scottish Election Survey 1997.

* *The pool of support for each party consists of those people who reported voting for the party in the 1997 general election and also people who gave that party as their second preference. Thus the columns are not mutually exclusive: the degree of overlap is shown in Table 3.3.*

Notes on coding of response categories:

[1] *percentage choosing 'definitely should' or 'probably should' (other categories being 'doesn't matter either way', 'probably should not' and 'definitely should not').*

[2] *percentage choosing 'agree strongly' or 'agree' (other categories being 'neither agree nor disagree', 'disagree' and 'disagree strongly').*

[3] *The options offered against this were 'Government should reduce taxes and spend less on health, education and social benefits' and 'Government should keep taxes and spending at the same level as now'.*

[4] *The option offered against this was 'The British government should not sign up to the Social Chapter because it would cost too many British workers their jobs'.*

[5] *The option offered against this was 'There should be no minimum wage because a minimum wage set by law would cost too many low paid workers their jobs'.*

[6] *The options offered against this were 'There should be more privatisation of companies by government' and 'Things should be left as they are now'.*

they come closer to the Conservatives. People close to the Liberal Democrats are more liberal than people close to Labour or the SNP in relation to stiffer sentences for criminals, to taxing cars for environmental purposes and to increasing aid for the developing world.

The evidence from the election survey, then, is that Labour and SNP sympathisers are almost identical in their views on policy, and that Conservative sympathisers are quite out of line with the common Scottish mood. On the basis of this analysis, we would expect the main policy conflict in Scottish politics to be between Labour and the SNP, and we would also conclude that the Conservative Party will find it very difficult to break out of a ghetto.

As well as analysing likely flows of voters, we can also ask explicitly how people would intend to vote in elections to the Scottish Parliament. This was done in the Scottish Referendum Study. The results were 13 per cent for the Conservatives, 54 per cent Labour, eight per cent Liberal Democrat, and 24 per cent SNP. Thus, even as early as just after the referendum, there was already evidence of a shift towards the SNP (something which, as we noted in Chapter One, became more pronounced in opinion polls in early 1998). Table 7.7 shows where these votes came from: whereas 98 per cent of Conservative votes for the Scottish Parliament would come from people who recalled having already voted Conservative in the 1997 general election, only 81 per cent of SNP votes would come from SNP voters in the general election. The proportion for the Liberal Democrats is even lower (73 per cent), and for Labour is similar to that for the Conservatives (94 per cent).

Table 7.7: **Intended vote in elections to the Scottish Parliament by vote in 1997 general election**

| | *intended vote in Scottish Parliamentary elections* | | | |
vote in 1997	Conservative	Labour	Lib Dem	SNP
Conservative	98	2	12	0
Labour	1	94	14	15
Lib Dem	0	1	73	4
SNP	0	3	1	81
Other	1	0	0	0
N (=100%)	88	314	47	131

Source: Scottish Referendum Survey 1997.

Excludes 92 people who would not report how they intended to vote in elections to the Scottish Parliament, and four who said they would vote for some other party. The balance of the percentages in each column consists of people who did not vote in the 1997 general election or who would not report how they had voted.

What is likely to influence people in deciding how to vote in elections to the Scottish Parliament? We test four types of explanation. The first set are the policy expectations which people have of the Parliament, and the second are the expectations about democratic effectiveness. In other words, do people who have optimistic expectations about the Parliament tend to vote in any particular way? The third is expectations which people have about Scottish independence and their attitudes to it: are people who expect or want the Parliament to lead Scotland to independence more or less likely to vote for the SNP (which supports that goal) or for its opponents (who do not). The fourth explanation is vaguer, less explicitly related to particular policies or outcomes: it is whether people trust the various parties to stand up for Scotland's interests. Does such general faith in Scottish parties better explain voting intentions than more detailed and possibly more rational considerations of policy or long-term goals?

The results of logistic regressions are summarised in Table 7.8. It shows the variables which were independently influential on each of the intended votes. There are two main points to notice. The first is that, in each case, trusting the party to stand up for Scottish interests is influential. Moreover, in details not shown in the table we find that this was by far the most influential factor, explaining more of the decisions to support a party than any rival variable. Thus part of the explanation for the deep unpopularity of the Conservatives in Scotland is simply that very few people trust them to work in Scotland's interests: see Table 7.9. For the Conservatives, we looked at this in Table 4.8, but using the Scottish Election Survey not the Referendum Survey. Comparing the two tables, we see that – if anything – the Conservatives were actually less trusted in the autumn of 1997 than in the summer (56 per cent in the autumn saying they would trust the Conservatives 'almost never' compared to 52 per cent in the summer). The Liberal Democrats do not do very well in this respect either. Similar majorities, however, trust Labour and the SNP to work in Scotland's interests, but the SNP has substantially more people than Labour who trust the party almost all the time.

Table 7.8:   **Models of intended vote in elections to the Scottish   Parliament**

---

intended vote in Scottish Parliamentary elections

Conservative	Labour	Lib Dem	SNP
Scottish Parliament's effect on NHS		Scottish Parliament's effect on NHS	
	Scottish Parliament's effect on taxes		Scottish Parliament's effect on taxes
Scottish Parliament's effect on Scotland's voice in the UK			
	Scottish Parliament's effect on people's say in government		
		Scottish Parliament's effect on Scotland's voice in the EU	Scottish Parliament's effect on Scotland's voice in the EU
	attitude to independence	attitude to independence	attitude to independence
trust Conservatives to work in Scotland's interests	trust Labour to work in Scotland's interests	trust Liberal Democrats to work in Scotland's interests	trust SNP to work in Scotland's interests

[Notes for Table 7.8 on next page]

Notes for Table 7.8:

Source: Scottish Referendum Survey 1997.

The table shows only those variables which were independently associated with at least one of the types of voting in a multiple logistic regression. The full set of variables which was tested for inclusion were the expectations of the Scottish Parliament's effect on policy (see Table 6.2 in Chapter Six), expectations of the democratic effectiveness of the Parliament (see Table 7.1), expectations of whether Scotland will become independent (see Table 7.3), attitudes to independence (first two response categories in Table 7.4) and trust in the parties to work in Scotland's interests (see Table 7.9 below). The direction of association with intended vote is discussed in the text.

Table 7.9: **Trust in the parties to work in Scotland's interests**

| | *party* | | | |
	Conservative	Labour	Lib Dem	SNP
Just about always	2	11	2	28
Most of the time	8	49	26	34
Only sometimes	33	36	61	27
Almost never	56	4	11	11
N (=100%)	674	674	674	674

Source: Scottish Referendum Survey 1997.

Excludes two people who did not reply.

Full wording was: 'How much do you trust ... to work in Scotland's interests?'.

The second main point is that attitudes to Scottish independence clearly separate SNP from Labour and Liberal Democrat voters: people who are in favour of independence (the first two categories shown in Table 7.4) are more likely than others to intend to vote SNP, and less likely to intend to vote Labour or Liberal Democrat. This tends further to confirm that attitudes to independence will become one of the main issues in Scottish politics.

But other variables do have some effect, probably reflecting the campaigning which the parties did during the referendum (see Chapters One, Two and Six). Voting Conservative is more likely among people who did not expect the Parliament to improve the health service than among people who were optimistic in this respect. The same is true of people who did not expect the Parliament to give Scotland a stronger voice in the UK. Having faith in the Parliament's capacity to improve the health service had the opposite effect on the Liberal Democrat vote: optimists are more likely to vote for them than pessimists. But, on the Parliament's effects on giving Scotland a stronger voice in the EU, pessimists are more likely to vote Liberal Democrat (and so they are not reflecting the party line).

Voting Labour or SNP is associated with expecting taxes not to go up under the Parliament. Thus, if these parties do try to use the Parliament's taxation powers, then – as we argued in Chapter Six – they will have to persuade voters that the money is being well spent on improving social policy.

People who expected the Parliament to give Scots a greater say in government are more likely to vote Labour than people who did not. Setting this alongside the clear distinction in attitudes to independence between the supporters of Labour and the SNP, we have a neat summary of these parties' positions on the new Parliament. Labour has argued that it is justified in itself because it will make government more responsive; the evidence from the statistical modelling is that they attract votes on the basis of that claim. The SNP argue that it should acquire greater powers; the same statistical models suggest that they, too, attract votes as a result. In contrast to the Liberal Democrats, they also attract votes from people who expect the Parliament to give Scotland a stronger voice in the EU, perhaps because the party has linked its support for independence with a more favourable attitude to the EU than either the Conservatives or Labour.

CONCLUSION

This analysis of people's expectations about the future of Scottish politics allows us to summarise the main points of the whole book, because these expectations have been influenced by all the factors which we have studied in earlier Chapters.

There are strong expectations of the Scottish Parliament, in relation both to policy and to democratic effectiveness. These expectations are quite evenly spread across social groups, and so can be said to be truly national. That explains the size of the majority in the referendum of 1997. Expectations for policy matter more than those for democracy, and both are more significant than any notion of the Parliament's expressing a sense of national identity, although the belief that the Parliament will produce good policy and responsive government does evidence some faith in Scottish institutions.

What happens after that might not be to the liking of its architects. Supporters of Scottish independence can employ two apparently contradictory arguments to push for more powers, and our analysis suggests that both will find significant support among the electorate. On the one hand, insofar as the Parliament does deal effectively with those areas for which it will be responsible, advocates of independence will be able to claim that this shows that Scots are well able to run their own affairs. On the other hand, if the Parliament fails to make an impact on matters – such as the performance of the economy – that are mostly reserved to Westminster, then the argument will also be put that this requires stronger powers in just those areas. The pressure to acquire such powers will be intensified by the fact that – as we saw in Chapter Five – Scots are more left-wing in several of these reserved areas than people in England. If the Parliament does, as a result of these pressures, evolve towards full independence, our evidence is that a clear majority of people in Scotland will not object. There is not yet a majority for independence, and so the SNP have a lot of work to do. But neither is there anything like the deep antipathy to independence as an ultimate goal which is expressed by Labour and Conservative politicians.

The outcome of these debates will depend on the party balance in the Parliament, and on relations with Westminster and the rest of the UK. The strongest determinant of voting will be perceptions of which party best represents Scotland's interests. The importance of representing these shows that matters of identity do remain relevant, even though they are not, in themselves, more important than more pragmatic matters such as the effectiveness of policy. What these interests are will be shaped partly by differences of values and policy preferences between Scotland and the rest of the UK. Our evidence from Chapters Four and Five is that, although Scotland shares in the broadly social democratic consensus that crosses the whole of Britain, it is more firmly to the left on some key areas. What is likely to be most significant for the future evolution of Scottish politics is that many of these areas are in matters that will be reserved to Westminster, such as redistribution of wealth and macro-economic policy. So, in due course, standing up for Scotland's interests is bound to require parties to seek greater powers for the Scottish Parliament.

As a result of this, there are two clear conclusions for the balance of parties in Scotland. The first is that the Conservatives remain in the ghetto into which they had gradually disappeared from the 1950s onwards, above all because they appeal to a small minority of firmly right-wing opinion. They have the image of not standing up for Scotland's interests. And they are saddled with the legacy of opposing the Parliament within which they will have to operate.

But, although the future of the Conservative Party may be the most important issue in British politics, it is a sideshow in Scotland compared to the battle between Labour and the SNP. They compete for the same left-of-centre votes; they each are trusted to work in Scotland's interests; and they each are enthusiastic about the new constitutional order. Although Labour may yet be able to claim credit for setting up the new Parliament, our evidence here suggests that the debate has already moved onto what that Parliament will do. The evidence from the surveys we have looked at suggests that Scots do not distinguish fundamentally between judging the effectiveness of policy and assessing the adequacy of the constitutional framework through which policy is made. Scots are not nationalists for expressive reasons: identity matters less to politics than effective government. But, equally, they are not anti-nationalist either. Because the option of independence will not go away – and because it does not provoke deep animosity among the majority – for the foreseeable future Scottish politics will continue to be dominated by the question of how the country is governed.

Appendix

THE DATA

The analysis in this book uses data gathered from various surveys of the electorate – the British Election Surveys of October 1974, 1979, 1987, 1992 and 1997, the Scottish Election Surveys of October 1974, 1979, 1992 and 1997, and the Scottish Referendum Survey of 1997. Full technical details of the surveys (both British and Scottish) up to 1992 can be found in, for example, Crewe et al (1995). For brevity in the text and the tables, we use the title 'British Election Survey' to subsume the Scottish ones.

The essential points about these surveys are:

- They were funded mainly by the Economic and Social Research Council, or its predecessor the Social Science Research Council. In 1997, the grant numbers were H552255004 for the Election Surveys and M543/285/001 for the Referendum Survey.
- The fieldwork was carried out by Social and Community Planning Research, London. The 1997 British and Scottish Election Surveys and the 1997 Scottish Referendum Survey were directed by the Centre for Research into Elections and Social Trends (CREST).
- The samples were chosen using random selection modified by stratification and clustering. Up to 1992, the sampling frame was the electoral register. In 1997, it was the Postcode Address File.
- The surveys were conducted by face-to-face interviews in people's homes, supplemented by a postal questionnaire which interviewees returned after the interview.
- The Scottish Election Surveys were based on a core of questions that was in common with the Britain-wide surveys, supplemented by questions specific to Scotland; extra people were interviewed in Scotland to bring the sample numbers up to around 800.

- The fieldwork took place during the two or three months after the election in question.
- The sample response rates in the Election Surveys were 74 per cent in 1974, 61 per cent in 1979, 70 per cent in 1987, 73 per cent in 1992 and 62 per cent in 1997. The response rate in the 1997 Referendum Survey was 69 per cent. Sample sizes are shown in the tables in the main text (as 'N').
- The data are weighted to make them representative of the known population characteristics.
- Data from all of the surveys is publicly available in the ESRC Data Archive at Essex University.

STATISTICAL SIGNIFICANCE

Because all the data come from samples, they are subject to sampling error. For many of the more complex analyses in the book, we have used statistical modelling to assess whether there is reliable evidence that particular variables are associated with each other. A summary of the meaning of such models is below, and the results are reported in the text and the tables in terms of statistical significance. This is best explained by an example. In Chapter Five (Table 5.1) we note that people in Scotland were more likely to be in favour of ending private education than people elsewhere in Britain. Specifically, 29 per cent of Scots held this view, but only about 20 per cent of people elsewhere. This difference is statistically significant at the one per cent level. What that means is that the chance of getting such a large observed difference in a sample of this size if there were truly no real difference between Scotland and the rest of Britain is just one in 100 (one per cent). Since that chance is small, we can safely conclude that the sample gives us evidence that there is such a real difference.

Although we have used modelling to check statistical significance, a rough rule of thumb is that – at the five per cent level of significance, and in a sample of size about 1000 – two sample proportions reflect a real difference if they differ by about three percentage points. If the relevant sample size is just 100, the observed difference would have to be about ten percentage points before we could say that it reflected a real difference.

MODELLING

Full technical details of the modelling we use can be found in many textbooks on social statistics, for example Aitkin et al (1988) and Bryman and Cramer (1997). All the statistical analysis was done using the computer package SPSS.

Ordinary and Logistic Regression

We use ordinary regression to model variables which have a continuous distribution. This is confined to the scales of political values dealt with in Chapter Four. Logistic regression is used to model variables which are dichotomous – for example, the decision to vote Yes or not to vote Yes on the first question in the referendum in 1997. The variable being modelled is called the dependent variable. The algebraic technicalities of these two types of regression differ quite a lot (and are explained by Aitkin et al (1988)), but the essential principles are the same: the idea is to assess whether a set of potential explanatory variables is influential on the dependent variable. For example, we ask in Chapter Six whether holding a sense of Scottish identity was influential on referendum vote. Most of the regression models we report involve several explanatory variables, and so are called multi-variate. For example, in Chapter Five (Table 5.2) we look at the simultaneous influence on attitudes to policy of sex, age, class, education, housing tenure, identity and living in Scotland. As discussed there, we find that apparent differences associated with living in Scotland are explained away when some of these other variables are put into the model. For example, different attitudes to nationalisation are explained by Scotland's having more council-house tenants than England.

Loglinear Modelling

For Table 5.1, we use loglinear modelling to investigate the associations among two or more variables each of which is measured as a set of categories: we are interested in whether the pattern of response to questions about policy differs between Scotland and the rest of Britain.

Selection of Variables

In several of the models, we tested for influential explanatory variables by the technique known as Forward Stepwise Selection (Draper and Smith, 1998). The essence of this technique is that it first chooses the explanatory variable that most strongly predicts the dependent variable, then, from those remaining, chooses the one that is the second-strongest predictor, and so on until there are no variables left which make a statistically significant difference to the dependent variable (at the five per cent level). In technical terms, the criterion on which the judgement of strength of prediction is based is the change in the value of the likelihood ratio.

References

Aitkin, M., Anderson, D., Francis, B. and Hinde, J. (1989), *Statistical Modelling in Glim*, Oxford University Press.

Anderson, B. (1983), *Imagined Communities: Reflections on the Origins and Spread of Nationalism*, London: Verso.

Barry, B. (1970), *Sociologists, Economists and Democracy*, London: Collier-Macmillan.

Benn, C. and Chitty, C. (1996), *Thirty Years On*, London: David Fulton.

Billig, M. (1995), *Banal Nationalism*, London: Sage.

Bochel, J. and Denver, D. (1992), 'The 1992 general election in Scotland', *Scottish Affairs*, no.1, autumn.

Boston, J. Levine, S., McLeay, E. and Roberts, Nigel S. (1997), 'The 1996 general election in New Zealand: proportional representation and political change', *Australian Quarterly*.

Brand, J., Mitchell, J. and Surridge P. (1993), 'Identity and the vote: class and nationality in Scotland', in *British Parties and Elections Yearbook 1993*, London: Frank Cass.

Brand, J., Mitchell, J. and Surridge, P. (1994), 'Social constituency and ideological profile: Scottish nationalism in the 1990s', *Political Studies*, 42.

Brand, J., Mitchell, J. and Surridge, P. (1995), 'Will Scotland come to the aid of the party?', in A. Heath, R. Jowell, and J. Curtice (eds), *Labour's Last Chance?: The 1992 Election and Beyond*, Aldershot: Dartmouth.

Brown, A. (1996), 'Women and politics in Scotland', in J. Lovenduski and P. Norris (eds), *Women in Politics* , Oxford University Press.

Brown, A. (1997), 'Scotland: paving the way for devolution?', *Parliamentary Affairs*, 50.

Brown, A., McCrone, D. and Paterson, L. (1996), *Politics and Society in Scotland*, London: Macmillan.

Brown, A., McCrone, D. and Paterson, L. (1998), *Politics and Society in Scotland*, London: Macmillan, second edition.

Bryman, A. and Cramer, D. (1997), *Quantitative Data Analysis*, London: Routledge.

Butler, D. and Kavanagh, D. (1997), *The British General Election of 1997*, London: Macmillan.

Butler, D. and Stokes, D (1969), *Political Change in Britain*, London: Macmillan.

Butler, D. and Stokes, D. (1974), *Political Change in Britain*, London: Macmillan.

Campbell, A., Converse, P., Miller, W. and Stokes, D. (1960), *The American Voter*, New York: Wiley.

Cohen, A.P. (1996), 'Personal nationalism: a Scottish view of some rites, rights, and wrongs', *American Ethnologist*, 23.

Converse, P (1964), 'The nature of belief systems', in D. Apter (ed.), *Ideology and Discontent*, New York: Free Press.

Crewe, I., Fox, A. and Day, N. (1995), *The British Electorate 1963-1992*, Cambridge University Press.

Curtice, J. (1988), 'One nation?', in R. Jowell, S. Witherspoon and L. Brook (eds), *British Social Attitudes the Ninth Report*, Aldershot: Dartmouth.

Curtice, J. (1996), 'One nation again?', in R. Jowell, J. Curtice, A. Park, L. Brook and K. Thomson (eds), *British Social Attitudes: the Thirteenth Report*, Aldershot: Gower.

Curtice, J. and Steed, M. (1997), 'Analysis of results', in D. Butler and D. Kavanagh, *The British General Election of 1997*, London: Macmillan.

Denver, D. (1994), '1994 European elections: results', *Scottish Affairs*, no.9, autumn.

Denver, D. (1997), 'The 1997 general election in Scotland: an analysis of the results', *Scottish Affairs*, no.20, summer.

Denver, D. and Bochel, H. (1995), 'Catastrophe for the Conservatives: the council elections of 1995', *Scottish Affairs*, no.13, autumn.

Dewar, D. (1998), 'The Scottish Parliament', in *Understanding Constitutional Change*, special issue of *Scottish Affairs*.

Dickson, T. (1989), 'Scotland is different, OK?', in D. McCrone, S. Kendrick and P. Straw (eds), *The Making of Scotland: Nation, Culture and Social Change*, Edinburgh University Press.

Downs, A. (1957), *An Economic Theory of Democracy*, New York: Harper.

Draper, N.R. and Smith, H. (1998), *Applied Regression Analysis*, New York: Wiley, third edition.

Dunleavy, P., Margetts, H. and Weir, S. (1997), *Devolution Votes: PR Elections in Scotland and Wales*, Democratic Audit Paper No.12.

Edwards, O.D. (ed.) (1989), *A Claim of Right for Scotland*, Edinburgh: Polygon.

Evans, G., Heath, A. and Lalljee, M. (1996), 'Measuring left-right and libertarian-authoritarian values in the British electorate', *British Journal of Sociology*, 47.

Feldman, S. (1988), 'Structure and consistency in public opinion – the role of core beliefs and values', *American Journal of Political Science*, 32.

Finlay, R.J. (1997), *A Partnership for Good? Scottish Politics and the Union Since 1880*, Edinburgh: John Donald.

Forsyth, M. (1995), 'The government of Scotland', speech on 30 November 1995 reprinted in L. Paterson (ed.) (1998), *A Diverse Assembly: the Debate on a Scottish Parliament*, Edinburgh University Press.

Gavin, N. and Sanders, D. (1997), 'The economy and voting', *Parliamentary Affairs*, vol.50, no.4.

Gellner, E. (1983), *Nations and Nationalism*, Oxford: Blackwell.

Hall, S. (1992), 'The question of cultural identity', in S. Hall, D. Held and T. McGrew (eds), *Modernity and Its Futures*, Cambridge: Polity.

Hall, S. and Held, D. (1989), 'Citizens and citizenship', in S. Hall and M. Jacques (eds), *New Times*, London: Lawrence and Wishart.

Harrop, M. and Miller, W. (1987), *Elections and Voters*, Basingstoke: Macmillan.

Heath, A., Evans, G. and Martin, J. (1994), 'The measurement of core beliefs and values', *British Journal of Political Science*, 24.

Heath, A., Jowell, R. and Curtice, J. (1985), *How Britain Votes*, London: Pergamon.

Heath, A., Jowell, R. and Curtice, J. (1987) 'Trendless fluctuation: a reply to Crewe', *Political Studies,* 35.

Heath, A., Jowell, R., Curtice, J. and Taylor, B. (1994), *Labour's Last Chance?*, Aldershot: Gower.

Heath, A., Jowell, R., Curtice, J., Evans, G., Field, J. and Witherspoon, S (1991), *Understanding Political Change*, London: Pergamon.

Heath, A. and Kellas, J. (1998), 'Nationalisms and constitutional questions', in *Understanding Constitutional Change*, special issue of *Scottish Affairs*.

Heath, A. and Park, A. (1998), 'Thatcher's children?', in R. Jowell, J. Curtice, A. Park, L. Brook, K. Thomson and C. Bryson (eds), *British Social Attitudes: the Fourteenth Report*, Aldershot: Gower.

Heath, A. and Taylor, B. (1996), 'British national sentiment', paper presented at the annual conference of the Political Studies Association, Glasgow, April.

Heath, A., Taylor, B., Brook, L. and Park, A. (forthcoming), 'British national sentiment', *British Journal of Political Science*.

Hobsbawm, E. (1990), *Nations and Nationalism since 1780: Programme, Myth and Reality*, Cambridge University Press.

Johnson, R., Pattie, C.J. and Allsopp, M.G. (1988), *A Nation Dividing? The Electoral Map of Great Britain, 1979-1987*, London: Longman.

Jones, P. (1997), 'Labour's referendum plan: sell-out or act of faith?', *Scottish Affairs*, no.18, winter.

Kellas, J. (1991), *The Politics of Nationalism and Ethnicity*, London: Macmillan.

Kinder, D. and Kiewit, D. (1981), 'Sociotropic politics: The American case', *British Journal of Political Science*, 11.

Lang, I. (1994a), 'Local government reform: change for the better', *Scottish Affairs*, no.9, autumn .

Lang, I. (1994b), 'Taking stock of taking stock', speech to Conservative Party Conference, Bournemouth, 12 October, reprinted in L. Paterson (1998) (ed.), *A Diverse Assembly: the Debate on a Scottish Parliament*, Edinburgh University Press.

Lynch, P. (1996a), 'The Scottish Labour Party: organisation, autonomy, ideology', paper presented to Elections, Public Opinion and Parties conference, University of Sheffield, 13-15 September.

Lynch, P. (1996b), 'The Scottish Constitutional Convention 1992-95', *Scottish Affairs*, no.15, spring.

Lynch, P. (1998), 'Third party politics in a four party system: The Liberal Democrats in Scotland', *Scottish Affairs*, no.22, winter.

MacWhirter. I. (1992), 'The disaster that never was: the failure of Scottish opposition after the 1992 general election', *Scottish Affairs*, no.1, autumn.

MacWhirter, I. (1995), 'Doomsday Two: the return of Forsyth', *Scottish Affairs*, no.13, autumn.

McAllister, I. and Rose, R. (1984) *The Nationwide Competition for Votes*, London: Frances Pinter.

McClosky, H. and Zaller, J. (1984), *The American Ethos: Public Attitudes towards Capitalism and Democracy*, Cambridge, Mass.: Harvard University Press.

McCrone, D. (1992), *Understanding Scotland*, London: Routledge.

McCrone, D. (1997), 'Opinion polls in Scotland, July 1996 – June 1997', *Scottish Affairs*, no.20, summer.

McCrone, D., Paterson, L. and Brown, A. (1993), 'Reforming local government in Scotland', *Local Government Studies*, 19.

Miller, W. (1981), *The End of British Politics? Scots and English Political Behaviour in the Seventies*, Oxford: Clarendon Press.

Mitchell, J. (1992), 'The 1992 election in Scotland in context', *Parliamentary Affairs*, 45.

Moreno, L. (1988) 'Scotland and Catalonia: the path to home rule', in D. McCrone and A. Brown (eds.) *The Scottish Government Yearbook,* Edinburgh: Unit for the Study of Government in Scotland.

Nairn, T. (1989), 'Tartan power', in S. Hall and M. Jacques (eds), *New Times*, London: Lawrence and Wishart.

Nairn, T. (1997), 'Sovereignty after the election', *New Left Review*, no.224.

Norris, P. (1997), 'The anatomy of a Labour landslide', *Parliamentary Affairs*, 50.

Norton, P. (1997), oral presentation to American Political Science Association Conference, Washington.

Paterson, L. (1994), *The Autonomy of Modern Scotland*, Edinburgh University Press.

Paterson, L. (1997), 'Student achievement and educational change in Scotland, 1980-1995', *Scottish Educational Review*, 29.

Paterson, L. (1998a), 'The Scottish Parliament and Scottish civil society: which side will education be on?', *Political Quarterly*, 69.

Paterson, L. (ed.) (1998b), *A Diverse Assembly: the Debate on a Scottish Parliament*, Edinburgh University Press.

Pattie, C., Denver, D., Mitchell, J. and Bochel, H. (1998), 'The 1997 Scottish referendum: an analysis of the results', *Scottish Affairs*, no.22, winter.

Pulzer, P. (1967), *Political Representation and Elections in Britain*, London: Allen and Unwin.

Rose, R. and McAllister, I. (1986), *Voters Begin to Choose*, London: Sage.

Sarlvik, B. and Crewe, I. (1983), *Decade of Dealignment*, Cambridge University Press.

Saunders, P. (1990), *A Nation of Home Owners?*, London: Unwin Hyman.

Scott, P.H. (1989), *Cultural Independence*, Edinburgh: Scottish Centre for Economic and Social Research.

Scottish Constitutional Convention (1995), *Scotland's Parliament, Scotland's Right*, Edinburgh: Convention of Scottish Local Authorities.

Scottish Office (1997), *Scotland's Parliament*, Cm.3658.

Seawright, D and Curtice, J (1995), 'The decline of the Scottish Conservative and Unionist Party 1950-1992: religion, ideology or economics?', *Contemporary Record* , 9.

Smith, A.D. (1991), *National Identity*, Harmondsworth: Penguin.

Surridge, P., Paterson, L., Brown, A. and McCrone, D. (1998), 'The Scottish electorate and the Scottish Parliament', in *Understanding Constitutional Change*, special issue of *Scottish Affairs*.

Zaller, J. (1992), *The Nature and Origins of Mass Opinion*, Cambridge University Press.

Index

177